T0105821

A Song from the Heart

The Pedagogical Philosophy
of Lorna Lutz Heyge, PhD

Jean Ellen Linkins, EdD

WESTBOW
P R E S S
A DIVISION OF THOMAS NELSON
& ZONDERVAN

Scripture quotations are from The Holy Bible, English Standard Version® (ESV®), copyright © 2001 by Crossway, a publishing ministry of Good News Publishers. Used by permission. All rights reserved.

WestBow Press books may be ordered through booksellers or by contacting:

WestBow Press
A Division of Thomas Nelson & Zondervan
1663 Liberty Drive
Bloomington, IN 47403
www.westbowpress.com
1 (866) 928-1240

Because of the dynamic nature of the Internet, any web addresses or links contained in this book may have changed since publication and may no longer be valid. The views expressed in this work are solely those of the author and do not necessarily reflect the views of the publisher, and the publisher hereby disclaims any responsibility for them.

Cover Graphic used by permission of Musikgarten/Music Matters, Inc.
507 North Arlington Street
Greensboro, NC 27406
1-800-216-6864 www.musikgarten.org

ISBN: 978-1-5127-1070-0 (sc)
ISBN: 978-1-5127-1072-4 (hc)
ISBN: 978-1-5127-1071-7 (e)

Library of Congress Control Number: 2015914366

Print information available on the last page.

WestBow Press rev. date: 10/28/2015

CONTENTS

LIST OF TABLES

DEDICATION

I dedicate this book to Lorna Heyge,
without whose loving efforts
to bring holistic music and literacy education
to the children,
the music education world
and those who teach and learn according to her work
would be without the richness of her synthesis
of the vast amounts of knowledge
she so wisely gathered together.
This rich synthesis
Lorna then carefully entrusted to us
to cherish and care for.
Thank you, Lorna.

If I speak in the tongues of men and of angels,
but have not love,
I am a noisy gong or a clanging cymbal.
And if I have prophetic powers,
and understand all mysteries and all knowledge,
and if I have all faith, so as to remove mountains,
but have not love,
I am nothing.
If I give away all I have,
and if I deliver up my body to be burned,
but have not love,
I gain nothing.
Love is patient and kind;
love does not envy or boast;
it is not arrogant or rude.
It does not insist on its own way;
it is not irritable or resentful;
it does not rejoice at wrongdoing,
but rejoices with the truth.
Love bears all things,
believes all things,
hopes all things,
endures all things.
Love never ends.
–1 Corinthians 13:1–3a (ESV)

FOREWORD

I had the great fortune to work with Lorna Heyge for almost 30 years, and watched her create ensembles everywhere—among her teacher trainees, with the children in her many classes, and between scholars in multiple fields. Sometimes these scholars came together in person or in the journal she created, and sometimes they just met in her mind. She was able to welcome everyone into the music, the discourse, or the musings.

Jean Ellen Linkins has created a remarkable book. She invites the reader to experience Lorna's amazing mind, tracing how it would expand with each opportunity in her life, always enlarging her vision as she incorporated what she learned from her classes with children and from the many fine thinkers she encountered. Her journey was an unusual blend—part destiny, part highly disciplined determination—and throughout, stunning creativity.

The author has offered us a ride through time in the mind of this true pioneer in early childhood music. And if that weren't enough, the book also provides the historic context behind this remarkable life journey, tracing the history of early childhood education, and highlighting the thoughts of other leaders in the fields of music, early childhood development, movement, and language.

While the book is a must-read for early childhood music educators, it would enrich any reader who loves children, values music or cares about enriching early childhood education.

Dee Joy Coulter, PhD

PREFACE AND ACKNOWLEDGMENTS

Seated at the roaring loom of time,
for six thousand years
man has woven a seamless garment.
But that garment is invisible and intangible
save where the dyes of written history fall upon it,
and forever preserve it
as a possession of generations to come.
—Allan Nevins, *The Gateway to History*, in Mark
1985, 29

I chose the quote above to open the preface because I love working with fabric and the embellishment of fabric (and so does Lorna Heyge, I discovered). I liked the thought of a "roaring loom of time" that is creating the great, invisible piece of the fabric of history—invisible except where some important historical occurrence has embellished it. Lorna Heyge's embellishment on this historical fabric is in the primary colors painted by the music of children, and the stitches have joyful sounds and dances and poems leaping from them above the surface.

This book originated as my doctoral dissertation on the subject of Lorna Heyge's pedagogical philosophy, which is a scholarly way of saying Lorna Heyge's philosophy—or how and what she thinks—about teaching. The bulk of this book has been adapted from that dissertation. Much of the scholarly approach has been eliminated (that is, the material that was required for a dissertation) or modified slightly to make the document more reader friendly. I elected to leave in the citations and references; references from the dissertation that only pertained to the scholarly portion have been eliminated from this book.

It is my prayer that the pages of this book will sing to you a new song—perhaps even an entire symphony—about the musical and educational promises for children that Lorna Heyge composed and brought to us all.

I acknowledge here, with gratitude difficult to express with enough jubilation, the assistance of the people who granted interviews for the original dissertation and those who read the manuscript for the book after it went through the metamorphosis from dissertation to book. The interviewees were Lorna Heyge, Audrey Sillick, Dee Joy Coulter, Robin Britt, Linda Robinson, Jill Hannagan, Karen McIver, Leilani Miranda, Cathy Mathia, Karen Haughey, Mary Louise Wilson, Joyce Jordan-DeCarbo, Amy Rucker, and Autumn Keller. The readers for the book version were Amalia Keleman, Sonya Glenning, and Amy Birney.

For the original work on the dissertation, many thoughtful and supportive friends came alongside to encourage my efforts. I will be eternally grateful to these friends: Donna Sheets, Nancy McPhee, Carolyn Ausborn, Amy Birney, Melissa Sheppard, Christa Habegger, and Sonya Glenning. The dissertation committee needs special recognition at this point as well: Dr. Dan Turner, Dr. Julie Hartman, and Dr. Michael Moore.

Our children, Michelle, Mandy, Jenny, and Erin, have stood by since 1996 while I went through the college woes for nearly twenty years! I am grateful that my dad, George B. Bush, and my "mom," Millie Frary Bush, are able to witness and cheer the completion of both the dissertation and the book. Millie's expertise as a librarian has been invaluable during the final proofing stage; I shall always cherish her help and her love.

My husband, Michael Linkins, through his unwavering faith in God as well as in me, deserves a gold medal for perseverance and stamina, a Cheerleader of the Millennia award, and my undying gratitude for his unfailing love and encouragement. I'm sure his "Mansion Over the Hilltop"[1] will have a grand studio where he

---

[1] "Mansion Over the Hilltop." Ira Stanphill/Singspiration Music/ ASCAP/SESAC

can play the best Martin guitar in heaven to his heart's content! There will also be the perfect worship venue for him to use God's gift of music that he loves so much.

My deepest gratitude does go to God for His Son, His love, lots of forgiveness, and several fresh starts. *Soli Deo gloria!*

INTRODUCTION

Early on, during my now thirteen years of teaching the *Musikgarten* curricula, I became aware of the educational treasure I held in my hands and used in my daily work. Actually, my daily work was and is hardly "work;" it is a manifestation of my love for the care and education of young children and for music—how natural it is to impart my love of music to the children in my care, as well as to their mothers, fathers, grandparents, siblings, and caregivers.

What led me to this joyful daily work happened when I was pursuing my Master of Music Education degree at the Eastman School of Music in my fifty-first year, for I came to college quite late in life. I believed at that time (2001), deep in my heart, that it was not for me to become a school teacher of high school or junior high school or even elementary school students (although I do teach all ages in the voice studio). But when my Eastman early childhood professor, Dr. Donna Brink Fox, brought out the first early childhood activity and we all sat on the floor and began that activity, I knew I had found the right age group for me. And when another Eastman professor, Dr. Richard Grunow, handed me a fresh-off-the-press copy of *Musikgarten Music Makers: At the Keyboard*, I knew I had found the right vehicle for me. And when my husband Mike and I made a trip to Greensboro that early winter of 2002 and spoke personally with Dr. Lorna Heyge, I knew I had found the right philosophy, as well as a lifework, for my teaching.

Over the years, I began studying Lorna Heyge's philosophy of teaching and discovered just how well-researched was her work. It was educationally as well as neurologically sound, and people would tell me that the story of the philosophy needed to be told—the music education world needed to know just what this pedagogy was really all about. So here we are—the dissertation was completed in 2012 and sits on library shelves; but the story is now in a format that is accessible to everyone.[2]

Welcome to the fascinating and brilliant work of Lorna Lutz Heyge, who loves music and who loves teaching music to children.

[2] The material for this book is adapted from the dissertation *The Pedagogical Philosophy of Lorna Lutz Heyge, PhD* (see References, Linkins, 2012).

CHAPTER ONE

EARLIEST YEARS—
LEADING TO THE PHILOSOPHY

Lorna Heyge's interest in early childhood music education developed quite gradually. Her particular path took her from a village in Upstate New York to a German community music school where she found her niche teaching music to young children.[3]

Before describing the curricula that Lorna Heyge developed, it seems appropriate to describe her life; knowing who Lorna Heyge is makes the history of her philosophy and her curricula more meaningful.

Early Life—The Village of Clyde, New York

During the middle years of the 1900s, Lorna's family lived in Clyde, New York, a village of about twenty-five hundred residents. Her father, Carl Martin Lutz, worked at the Hemingway and Co. canning factory in Clyde; and her mother, Grace Chamberlin Lutz, raised the children and enjoyed singing and playing the piano. Lorna's German grandparents, William and Johanna Lutz, lived in a nearby village. Lorna remembers her grandfather speaking

---

[3] Unless otherwise noted, all detail for Lorna Heyge's biography is derived from a personal interview with Lorna Heyge conducted on May 7, 2011.

German, although he died when she was a young child. Lorna later built upon her interest in the German language and culture during her college years and beyond.

Young Lorna helped with the family's finances by working as she could—in the summers at the canning factory and regularly as a pianist in the village. In such a small village, a talented pianist was often in demand, playing for everything from church services to Sunday school to Scouts. Lorna played piano for all the church denominations and found some success by experimenting on the organ, although she was studying only piano.

Lorna's earliest memory of playing an instrument other than piano is from second or third grade, when she learned to play the Tonette, a precursor to the recorder that is now popular as a first instrument for elementary students. Lorna began playing clarinet in third grade and was accepted into the high school band in the fifth grade. She likes to say with a smile that she ended up spending eight years in the high school band.

Lorna credits the New York State school system with having fine teachers in all subjects and at all levels. She believes music had a strong influence on her because of the music education she received in the public schools, although she admitted that her first interest in public school was mathematics.

There were only two piano teachers in the village; and in the confines of such a small geographic area, the two women were in competition. Lorna's mother had arranged for piano lessons with one of the teachers, who was a personal friend. But because they did not work well together, Lorna was relieved to have the lessons end when this particular teacher temporarily stopped teaching for medical reasons. Lorna received permission from her father to not go back to the first teacher; he arranged for her to study with the second teacher, with whom Lorna was a much better match. When it came time to think about college, this teacher encouraged Lorna to apply to both Syracuse University and to the Eastman School of Music of the University of Rochester. Both universities were a short distance from the Village of Clyde. Lorna had been particularly interested in studying math and wasn't sure she wanted to focus on piano. However, her father died in the spring of her senior year of high school. For financial reasons, the scholarship she was offered by the Eastman School made it the obvious choice.

The Eastman School of Music

Lorna, who had attended only one live concert in her life, now found herself, a brand-new college freshman, in the formidable polished-marble grand hall at the Eastman School of Music during orientation week. After witnessing some of the best-of-the-best stroll up to the grand hall's grand piano to show off their virtuosity, she made inquiry about changing her major. There was only one organ student at the Eastman School that year, so space was available for her in the organ department. Lorna thus had the opportunity to study for four years with world-renowned organist David Craighead. The change of focus from piano to organ, coupled with the rigorous education at the Eastman School, had a dramatic effect upon her life, moving her forward toward a forty-plus-year career in early childhood education.

As an undergraduate at the Eastman School, Lorna began German studies because of the influence of German composers on organ literature. Lorna's grandfather was German, so German seemed to be an appropriate language to study and enjoy for the required language component of her degree. She spent two summers at Middlebury College, Vermont, in an intensive German-language summer course. At Middlebury, she accompanied many musical events, including a required one-hour-per-day session of singing German folk-song literature. This focus on folk-song literature, along with her public-school experience, where folk music was an important part of the music education, helped solidify a love of folk music that remains with Lorna to this day. Lorna now has an extensive collection of folk music, collected gradually over time, which she has cataloged in a database according to range, meter, key, topic, and the song's possible function in a music lesson.

Exchange Student—Rochester to Cologne

Lorna became more interested in German studies while at the Eastman School; and in order to extend her education beyond what was available at the Eastman campus, she traveled to the main campus of University of Rochester for extra classes. Toward the end of Lorna's undergraduate studies, Dr. Kneisel at the Eastman School suggested to Lorna that she apply to compete for an exchange program between the University of Rochester and the University of Cologne in Germany. Because she was a music major rather than a German-studies major, Lorna was surprised and honored that she earned second place in the competition. The first-place competitor, usually a German-studies major, won the right to attend the University of Cologne; and the second-place competitor became the backup attendee, should the first-place competitor withdraw. With graduation approaching, Lorna applied to Northwestern University in Chicago for a master's degree and received a full scholarship. On graduation day from the Eastman School, however, Dr. Hanhart, the head of the German department for the University of Rochester, told her that the person who had won the exchange to Cologne decided to turn it down in favor of a scholarship to Yale. Lorna contacted Northwestern, who granted her an extension on her scholarship, allowing her to take part in the year-long exchange program with the University of Cologne.

In Cologne to study German language and literature, Lorna passed the entrance exams into the University of Cologne and then went to the University's Hochschule für Musik to seek out an organ teacher. The teacher there did not seem to be as challenging as Lorna had hoped; so she boarded a train for Frankfurt to interview with Helmut Walcha, an accomplished organist, who accepted her as a student.

Master's Degree—Northwestern

Upon completion of that exchange year, Lorna returned to the United States and attended Northwestern University. To help with living expenses, Lorna secured a job as church organist at a Lutheran church on the north side of Chicago. The church had a choir that sang in German for the German service and one that sang in English for the English service. While at Northwestern, Lorna studied with her third exemplary organ teacher, Grigg Fountain, a former student of Walcha.

Artist's Diploma/PhD—Cologne

At the completion of the master's degree at Northwestern, Lorna applied for and received the *Deutsche Akademischer Austausch Dienst* scholarship (literally, German Academic Exchange Service), a Fulbright award that was established by the German government as part of a way to thank the American government for assistance through the Marshall Plan in reconstruction following World War II. Lorna's award was to study organ, which she did with Michael Schneider, another fine organist, at the Hochschule für Musik in Cologne. As her studies progressed, Schneider advised Lorna that if she wanted to teach on the college level, she should speak with his doctoral advisor, Karl Gustav Fellerer, who was chair of the musicology department at Cologne. Soon thereafter, she enrolled as a PhD student in musicology. Lorna obtained a two-year extension from the German government, which gave her time to complete the academic studies.

Greensboro College—Professor of Organ Performance

Lorna now had a Master of Music from Northwestern University and both a PhD in Musicology and an Artist's Diploma in Organ from the University of Cologne. She returned to the United States, where college-teaching positions for organ had become scarce. Through prior connections, Lorna obtained a three-year teaching position at Greensboro College in North Carolina. During her first year at Greensboro, she taught twenty-one organ majors, eighteen of whom were doing recitals. That is a significant number and quite a pressure for a new college professor. She also taught church-music history and other subjects during this time.

CHAPTER TWO

THE DEVELOPMENT OF
LORNA HEYGE'S TEACHING PHILOSOPHY

Association of German Music Schools

In 1971, at the end of her three-year teaching term at Greensboro College, Lorna applied for work in Germany and had two possibilities: teach English in the schools or be a *stellvertretende Direktor*, or assistant director (Hannagan 2010), of a youth music school, part of the Association of German Music Schools. She chose the latter. This choice was another milestone in the development of her teaching philosophy, and it moved her toward early childhood education.

As assistant director of the school, Lorna took part in a growing movement in Germany to establish music schools for children in neighborhoods so that it was convenient for families to walk together to lessons. In her position, Lorna taught piano, recorder, and fundamental music courses for four- to six-year-old and seven- to nine-year-old children at various locations in Troisdorf. Sometimes the classrooms were in public school buildings—such was the cooperation between the public schools and the neighborhood music schools, indicating governmental support of music education. Other than previously teaching piano and Sunday school lessons to young children, this was Lorna's first early childhood education experience.

Curriculum Musikalische Früherziehung

The original German curriculum that Lorna taught, beginning in 1971, was the *Curriculum Musikalische Früherziehung*, a two-year program for four- to six-year-old children. This curriculum still exists in Germany under the title *Tina und Tobi*, published by Bosse Verlag GmbH and Company. The primary author of the program, Diethard Wucher, who first published the curriculum in 1968 (Wucher 1996), believed that there should be a youth music school in every neighborhood. Since 1971, other curricula have been created; but the *Curriculum Musikalische Früherziehung* has become the standard for all early childhood music curricula in Germany since that time. The name *Musikalische Früherziehung* remains the common name for any music class that four- and five-year old-children attend, regardless of the actual title of the curriculum taught.

Important considerations for the success of the neighborhood music school in Germany were that the schools were places where families could participate together and to which families could walk easily and safely. In 1971, the neighborhood music schools were accepted by the public and enjoyed by families. The schools continue to thrive to this day.

From Organ Performance to Early Childhood Music

By accepting the job in Germany in 1971, Lorna stepped off of the path of teaching organ on the college level (Hannagan 2010). As she taught the young children, Lorna could see solutions to musical problems she had witnessed in the college-aged students (Hannagan 2010). This discovery deepened her interest in early childhood music pedagogy.

After a year of teaching in the German music schools, Lorna briefly returned to the United States on a holiday; and in casual conversation, she discussed her work with colleagues. As they all talked about their lines of work, Lorna realized that nothing like this German music program was being taught in the United States on a large scale. Upon her return to Germany, Lorna approached Wucher about the possibility of doing an English-language adaptation of the program.

By now, the program was well accepted in Germany. Wucher was about to undertake a large, national research project to further improve and develop the *Curriculum Musikalische Früherziehung* and invited Lorna to participate in the project. There was a team of about thirty teachers, in addition to Wucher and specialists in listening and other categories. Each teacher taught at least two classes. Lorna taught two in German and, having translated the curriculum herself, two in English. The teachers were trained in the proper methods of observation, and they reported their observations made during classes. There were additional observers who regularly took notes, made audio recordings of every lesson, and made video recordings of every sixth lesson. There were meetings approximately every six weeks for the teachers to discuss their work and various revisions that were being made.

In 1973 (Hannagan 2010), Lorna was asked to do an English-language adaptation of the curriculum, which included cultural adaptations; she taught those first classes to English-speaking children in Bonn. There were two classes of twelve children, and Lorna made the curriculum adaptations as the classes progressed. Her experience in teaching the curriculum in German enabled the process of adapting while teaching to go smoothly. Lorna translated some German songs into English and substituted some English-language songs, thus beginning to make the adaptation culturally relevant to English-speaking children and families. Lorna realized that cultural relevance was an important ingredient to the children's learning process. A second edition of the *Curriculum Musikalische Früherziehung* was published in 1974 (Wucher 1996). Also in 1974, at the end of that year of teaching the children in Bonn, Wucher decided that the adaptation should be tested in the United States.

CHAPTER THREE

EARLY CHILDHOOD MUSIC COMES TO THE UNITED STATES

The Original *Kindermusik,* 1974-1994

Lorna returned to the United States in 1974 and began to teach the adapted music program at Greensboro College. She called this program *Kindermusik* (L. Heyge, personal communication, May 7, 2011). Lorna continued to work on the English-language adaptation, making culturally relevant substitutions of song literature and illustrations. The new adaptations were then published in 1978. The program was well received, and classes filled quickly. Within the first year, families began requesting similar courses for their six- to eight-year-old children; Lorna then developed these additional courses. The program was going well. But after three years, Greensboro College needed Lorna's teaching space in order to do some renovations; so the music classes moved to the church where Lorna was organist.

The First Teacher-Trainer Workshop

In 1974, the student MENC (The Music Educator's National Conference[4]) group at Greensboro College asked Lorna to be their speaker at the state conference. Linda Robinson attended that conference and afterward contacted Lorna to find out more about the Kindermusik program. Lorna invited Linda to observe a class at Greensboro. Linda then received training from Lorna at the first Kindermusik teacher-training workshop, which was held in 1975 (Hannagan 2010). This was the only teacher-training workshop in Lorna's history to not include a demonstration class of children. Every teacher-training workshop since then has included a demonstration class so that the teachers in training are able to observe in practice what they are learning at the workshop. Linda soon opened her own studio and became one of the first trained teachers to assist Lorna with the teacher-training conferences. At the time of this writing, Linda continues to teach classes and to work closely with Lorna.

Toronto, Canada

In 1978, Lorna married Hermann Heyge and moved to Toronto, Canada, where her German-born husband worked. This move headed Lorna in the direction of another major milestone in the development of her teaching philosophy and the path of her early childhood education career.

As Toronto, Canada, and Rochester, New York, are within driving distance of each other, Lorna reacquainted herself with David Craighead, her organ professor at the Eastman School, and resumed organ lessons. Within a year of her arrival in Toronto,

---

[4]   The organization now known as NAfME has experienced several name changes since its formation: "We were originally called Music Supervisors National Conference, then Music Educators National Conference (MENC), then MENC: The National Association for Music Education. On September 1, 2011, we became simply National Association for Music Education." Retrieved March 9, 2012, from http://www.menc.org/about/

her organ professor from Cologne, Germany, asked her to meet another former organ student of his who was living in Toronto. This man, who had studied music in Germany, and his wife, who had been a choral director in Germany and was aware of early childhood music education there, knew Lorna had taught the *Curriculum Musikalische Früherziehung* program in Germany. They convinced Lorna to open a class for their daughter (Heyge 2011). The class drew the immediate attention of families because there was no other instruction like it in Toronto at the time. It was not long before Lorna had many more requests for classes.

Audrey Sillick and the Montessori Experience

At some point around 1980, Lorna's Kindermusik classes came to the attention of Helma Trass, the principal of the Toronto Montessori School, through the recommendation of a board member whose son was in one of Lorna's classes. After observing Lorna teach, Trass was impressed enough to invite Lorna to teach music classes at that particular Montessori school. Incorporating music classes outside of the official AMI (*Association Montessori Internationale*) curriculum was a major move for the school, as they and the Montessori Teacher Training Institute were quite strict about remaining pure to the teachings of Montessori.

Soon Lorna became acquainted with Audrey Sillick, founder and director of the Montessori Teacher Training Institute since 1971; and thus began a friendship and educational partnership that remained strong until Audrey passed away in 2014.

> I was fortunate ... to be introduced to the world of child development through Audrey Sillick, a well-known Montessori Teacher Trainer, but more significantly, a woman of great wisdom about young children and how they learn. In 12 years of working with her in Canada, I learned about children and came to a much better understanding of the significant role music should play in the

total development of children. (Heyge in Johnson 2006, 34)

At the Institute, Audrey gave lectures that Lorna attended; and although the lectures did not pertain to music, Lorna could see where Audrey's knowledge of child development meshed with Lorna's view of teaching young children and could have direct bearing on her music curriculum. Lorna's philosophy of how to teach music was already broad-based due to her rigorous music education and her experience with the *Curriculum Musikalische Früherziehung* as well as *Kindermusik,* her English-language adaptation. Lorna could see the benefit of combining her pedagogy with Audrey's knowledge and similar love of teaching young children. It was not long before they began working together on the curriculum, blending Audrey's developmental knowledge with Lorna's musical knowledge, and creating a curriculum that addresses the needs of the whole child. Audrey's teaching philosophy was rooted not only in Montessori's principles but also in a deep respect for nature and science, and these areas were likewise brought into the curriculum and woven into Lorna's teaching philosophy.

Audrey's knowledge of child development and learning exerted a lasting and dramatic influence on Lorna's teaching philosophy, as will be described later. Their meeting and combining their considerable gifts had a significant effect on the formation of Lorna's philosophy and her lifework.

The Core Group of Teacher-Trainers

In 1981, Karen McIver attended a Kindermusik teacher-trainer conference held at Westminster Choir College, where she received training from Lorna and subsequently opened her own Kindermusik studio. Karen soon joined Linda as a teacher-trainer of the Kindermusik program. Others followed: Leilani Miranda in 1985, Joyce Jordan-DeCarbo and Mary Louise Wilson in 1986, Amy Rucker in 1989, Cathy Mathia in 1990, Karen Haughey in 1992, Jill Hannagan in 1995, and Autumn Keller in 2001. These became the teacher-trainers selected and entrusted by Lorna to impart her broad-based program, and most important, her specific philosophy of teaching, to new teachers of her curriculum. The teacher-trainers conduct training workshops for prospective teachers every summer and at various times and locations throughout the year. As of 2012, several of the teacher-trainers have also conducted workshops in Korea, Malaysia, Taiwan, China, New Zealand, South Africa, and Germany.[5]

Birth of the Kindermusik Teachers Association

In 1984, the first meeting of Kindermusik teachers was held. The location for this first event was Lorna's backyard garden in Toronto. There was a tour of the Montessori school led by Audrey, a talk by Lorna, and excellent bratwurst, homemade by Hermann Heyge (Heyge, personal communication May 7, 2011). Subsequent meetings were held every two years; and from this first meeting, the Kindermusik Teachers Association was born.

The Need for a New Curriculum

In the early days of the *Kindermusik* curriculum, Lorna personally trained prospective teachers. As she was conducting one such teacher-training workshop in 1985, she realized that, because of her integration of the Montessori principles through Audrey's teachings, and the integration of knowledge she had acquired by attending conferences on various aspects of cognition and psychology, her philosophy of teaching had changed greatly since the 1978 curriculum publication. She was no longer referring to the 1971 and 1978 published materials (Heyge 2011). At that point

---

[5] Musikgarten, as of this 2015 writing, now has classes for children in Australia, Austria*, Canada*, China*, France, Germany*, Great Britain, Hong Kong*, India*, Indonesia*, Malaysia*, New Zealand, Philippines, Singapore*, South Africa, South Korea*, Spain, Thailand*, and Taiwan*. *In those locations marked with an asterisk, teacher-training workshops are also conducted. Retrieved May 25, 2015 from www.musikgarten.org.

she knew it was time to rewrite the curriculum entirely rather than write a revision. She approached the German publisher, who initially agreed, but then was unable to meet Lorna's time element (Heyge 2011). Lorna therefore sought a new publisher in the United States. The new edition of the *Kindermusik* curriculum, now free of copyright restrictions, was written by Lorna and Audrey, field-tested by Linda, and published in 1988.

The Teachings of Ed Gordon

In the late 1980s, another meeting occurred that created further change in Lorna's philosophy, and this was her introduction to the teachings of Dr. Edwin Gordon through Joyce Jordan-DeCarbo in Miami. Gordon, a musician and music education researcher, had developed an approach to teaching music that paralleled the way children learn language. (Gordon's approach is explained later in this book.)

By the mid-1980s, Gordon's *Music Learning Theory* had gained some, although not widespread, acceptance among music educators. In 1986, having heard of Lorna's work and wanting to be trained in the program, Joyce invited Lorna to the University of Miami where Joyce was teaching early childhood music classes. Joyce and Mary Louise Wilson, who was teaching in Joyce's program at the University, were both trained by Lorna in Mary Louise's living room (M. L. Wilson, personal communication, n.d.). At this meeting, Joyce, who had studied with Ed Gordon, introduced Lorna to the work of Gordon. In particular, Gordon's unique system of tonal and rhythm patterns as building blocks of music literacy—much like patterns of letters are building blocks of language literacy—was intriguing to Lorna. By 1994, Lorna and Audrey wove Gordon's work into the entire curriculum.

The Kindermusik Teachers Association (KTA)

In 1986, the Kindermusik Teachers Association was officially formed. Members of this growing group of people, trained by

Lorna to teach the Kindermusik program, had expressed a desire to come together and share their experiences. The first formal meeting was held in Winston-Salem, North Carolina, and was chaired by the first president, Linda Robinson. The focus of this first meeting was the formation of the Association and the logistics of getting everyone together to learn from each other. Subsequent meetings were held every two years. In 1988, the new Heyge/Sillick curriculum was the focus of the meeting, and the president was Leilani Miranda.[6] In 1990, under President Cathy Mathia, the meeting was held in Estes Park, Colorado; Dee Coulter was an invited speaker. The 1992 meeting under President Barb Toth[7] was held in Chicago and featured Dee and piano pedagogue Paul Pollei, among others.

Dee Joy Coulter

Another milestone in Lorna's journey occurred in 1990 when she became acquainted with Dee Joy Coulter, a neurological researcher, author, and college instructor with a keen interest in child development. In 1985, Dee was invited to participate in an Orff summer teacher-training workshop following her 1982 article in the Orff journal entitled "Brain's Timetable for Developing Musical Skills." Following that article and workshop, Lorna invited Dee to speak at the 1990 Kindermusik Teachers Association meeting. To prepare for that meeting, Dee read the work of Lorna and Audrey and, although not a musician herself, was impressed by the broad scope and the depth of their work (Coulter, personal communication, August 9, 2010). Dee joined with Lorna and Audrey, adding a new dimension to workshops and to the creative processes at work in Lorna's early childhood teaching philosophy and her program. Dee made a point of saying that from her earliest connection to the work of Lorna and Audrey, she was impressed at their "deep systems understanding. It had such coherence and integrity to what was being said … it was the

---

[6] and [7]Name of president supplemented from http://www.ecmma.org/resources/history/. Retrieved February 4, 2012.

distilled essence of a way to see the world" (D. Coulter, personal communication, August 9, 2010).

> It seemed to me, when I read their work, that there is a level of scholarly integrity to the design. Lorna designed a lot of it, she sought scholarly input for it, and saw a big enough picture to make sure that there was a coherence between the musical curriculum, the developmental fit, the social-emotional aspects, and the pre-literacy exposures. (Coulter, personal communication, August 9, 2010)

The Year of Change

The year 1994 was a time of change for Lorna. She had decided to take on partners in the Kindermusik business. These partners were to have handled the business side of things, and she would be free to handle the education side—education was and is of first importance to Lorna. However, the two partners decided to sell the trademark—the name Kindermusik—thus making the company a commercial enterprise, which was not Lorna's intent for her work. At that point, Lorna separated from the company and resumed her original path, which remains focused on education, under the new company named Musikgarten/Music Matters, Inc.

KTA to ECMMA

The 1994 convention of the Kindermusik Teachers Association was already scheduled to be held in Asheville. As a result of Lorna's split with the Kindermusik brand name, the KTA Board, with the vote of the membership, decided to change the name of the association so that its designation would better represent a group who came together to learn and share educational information rather than a group who met under a commercial trademark. At that meeting, the name was changed to ECMA—the Early Childhood Music

Jean Ellen Linkins, EdD

Association. In 1998[8] the name changed to ECMMA—the Early Childhood Music and Movement Association—in order to include movement, which is a major aspect of early childhood music education.

---

[8] Year of name change from ECMA to ECMMA was retrieved February 4, 2012, from http://www.ecmma.org/resources/history/

CHAPTER FOUR

MUSIKGARTEN–FROM 1994 FORWARD

Musikgarten

Lorna established *Musikgarten* in 1994 with a completely new curriculum, co-written by Lorna and Audrey. Because it was no longer associated with the original German curriculum or publisher, Lorna could add the theories of Gordon, including the sound-before-sight approach, and more fully incorporate Audrey and Dee's influences. She now had the freedom to focus on her educational goals, dropping some things from the German curriculum that were no longer useful but had been kept in place because of copyright issues.

Foundation for Music-Based Learning

In 1993, Lorna established the Foundation for Music-Based Learning (Heyge 1995b). Under the Foundation, Lorna began the *Early Childhood Connections* journal, edited by Martha Hallquist, which was published from 1995 until 2005. Through the vehicle of the journal, Lorna's purpose was to bring together all of the prominent early childhood music and education authors, researchers, and others who would then have an audience of people, including practitioners in the field, interested in early childhood music and education. Her intent was to have a community, free from all trademark boundaries, open for the exchange of ideas, and not serving any agenda except the dissemination of ideas and research findings.

For the final issue of the journal in 2005, Lorna wrote "an open letter to readers from ECC publisher, Lorna Heyge" (Heyge 2005). She said:

> With your help, we have met our goals of establishing connections within our field, as well as to the music education and early childhood communities, to the music therapy and special education communities, and to the academic and research communities. (Heyge 2005)

Lorna cited the need "to find ways to educate more teachers and parents, as well as the policy makers who make decisions for children … [We] must look for current avenues that will reach more people" (Heyge 2005). She said the Foundation would look to publish advocacy and educational documents as well as look toward research opportunities. She closed the letter by saying:

> We have held true to our goal to "use this forum to share our knowledge, to define what we have in common, to examine new viewpoints, and to clarify goals for the children in our care." (Heyge 2005)

After closing the journal, the Foundation began supporting the Music for Learning program, created by Linda Robinson together with Lorna, and administered by Linda. This program brings experienced Musikgarten teachers into child-development centers serving four-year-old children of low socio-economic status who are not able to participate in Musikgarten classes due to financial constraints. The purpose of Music for Learning is to help prepare the children in their year before kindergarten through musical activities that enhance their readiness for school. Such work has been a passion of Lorna's since she taught in Robin Britt's Project Uplift outreach program in Greensboro in 1991 (L. Heyge, personal communication, May 7, 2011; L. Robinson, personal communication, June 6, 2011).

Continuing the Journey of Educational Focus

In 2007, Lorna, President of Musikgarten, promoted long-time trainer and keyboard co-author Jill Hannagan to the position of Executive Vice President of Musikgarten, and twelve-year employee Jeff Spickard to Administrative Vice President of the company. In 2015, Jill chose to return to focus on her highly successful Musikgarten studio and continue as a Musikgarten teacher-trainer. Jeff was promoted to President of Musikgarten, with Lorna as the Chief Executive Officer. The changes in administrative structure since 2007 have enabled Lorna to spend time in program development as well as in semi-retirement enjoying bicycling and travel with her husband Hermann. As of the writing of the dissertation (completed in 2012), Lorna continued to attend conferences, maintain dialogs with Audrey, Dee, and Robin Britt, and exchange ideas and experiences with her teacher-trainers on a regular basis. She is an internationally respected speaker and is well known for having a high level of determination and passion for educating young children from all walks of life.

CHAPTER FIVE

THE SCAFFOLDING THAT UNDERGIRDS THE *MUSIKGARTEN* CURRICULA

The Framework of the Philosophy

The educational framework of Lorna's philosophy of teaching[9]—the educational theories that form the scaffolding or skeleton of her unique work—is rooted in the ideas of historical early childhood education pioneers Comenius, Rousseau, Pestalozzi, and Froebel, all of whom recognized the need for distinct education for very young children (Heyge 1999). Their ideas are the basic foundation for much of the work done in the field of early childhood education.

Twentieth-century theorists of educational psychology (Piaget and Montessori), music (Orff and Kodály), and movement (Laban and Dalcroze), whom Lorna referred to as "great masters" (Heyge 1999), have specific influence on her teaching philosophy, each in their respective fields, as follows:

Piaget's theories of stages of development and order of information processing are exhibited by the age divisions of Musikgarten's courses for children ages birth through nine (see table 1). Montessori's theories that a child should have sensory experience prior to cognitive comprehension, that there is a hidden nature of a child, and that we should follow the leading of the child are exhibited by the teaching artistry Lorna conveys at workshops

---

[9] Information based upon Heyge 1999.

and in teacher's guides and parent communications. The idea of Dalcroze that children can learn elements of music through movement is visible in activities in the lesson plans throughout the curricula. Laban's idea of movement elements of weight-space-time-flow with music added to the motions is visible in activities in the lesson plans throughout the Musikgarten courses. Orff's use of rhythm instruments and formation of ensembles is visible in the use of the instruments and in ensemble development activities in the *Music Makers* series. Kodály's ideas of the importance of folk music, the movable-do *solfège* system, his sequence of learning, and the theory of sound before sight are visible throughout the *Musikgarten* curricula from the earliest level onward.

These influences are further refined by Lorna's assimilation of the ideas of contemporaries[10] Audrey Sillick and Dee Joy Coulter, the approach of Ed Gordon, and Lorna's ongoing integration of information from conferences on cognition, psychology, and education-related matters (Heyge 2011), summarized as follows:

Audrey Sillick, co-author of all *Musikgarten* curricula, contributed Montessori teachings, a way of being with the child, and a strong focus on nature; these are exhibited by Lorna and teacher-trainers at workshops and are visible in content and manner of communications to teachers and to parents. Dee Joy Coulter contributed knowledge of neurological functions and of the brain's timetable for music and learning, which are exhibited by Lorna and the teacher-trainers at workshops, as well as through publications for teachers and parents and contributions to curricula. Ed Gordon contributed the importance of tonal and rhythm patterns as building blocks of music, the idea that music learning parallels language learning, and a timetable for music learning in his *Music Learning Theory*, all of which are visible throughout the Musikgarten courses.

---

[10] As the scaffolding is explained, there will be some overlap of information covered in the biographical discussion.

Pre-Twentieth Century Education Theorists

In the 1999 quarterly *Musikgarten Messenger*, on the occasion of her twenty-fifth anniversary in the field of early childhood music education, Lorna (1999) wrote a concise history of her philosophical journey.[11] As a prelude to that history, Lorna briefly summarized the history of early childhood education by listing the following early advocates:[12]

John Amos Comenius (1592–1670)

Comenius was perhaps the first modern-era advocate of preschool education. He wrote *The Great Didactic* (1659), wherein he stated his belief that "not only was there an identifiable stage of growth from infancy to six years of age, but also that there was an appropriate curriculum for this age" (Weiser 1982 in McDonald and Simons 1989, 5). According to Morrison, Comenius believed "humans are born in the image of God" and by education are "to fulfill this godlike image" (Morrison 2004, 82). Education should begin early, "while tender" (Comenius, in Morrison 2004, 82). He believed that the mother at home could impart to the young child "factual, language, and sensory skills" (McDonald and Simons 1989, 5).

Lorna's teaching philosophy embraces the Comenius ideal of having a curriculum for the age range of infancy to age six. Although initially teaching the German curriculum that served children ages four to six, Lorna's philosophy transitioned through her work with Audrey, expanding her belief to encompass the need for education that begins at birth. The *Musikgarten* curricula addresses music education for children ages birth through nine years of age.

---

[11] The Kindermusik/Musikgarten archival data studied for the dissertation research included a twenty-first year synopsis of Lorna's work.

[12] For the benefit of the reader, I have enhanced Lorna's brief descriptions of the educational theories for clarity with respect to her work as well as to music education history.

Jean-Jacques Rousseau (1712–1778)

Rousseau, author of *Emile* and *The Social Contract* (both published in 1762), advocated "natural experiences in a natural environment, with minimal interference from adults" (McDonald and Simons 1989, 6). Rousseau's "concept of natural unfolding echoes Comenius's concept of naturalness and appears in current programs that stress promoting children's readiness as a factor in learning," (Morrison 2004, 85) which is echoed by Piaget's stages of development theory, Montessori's principles, and Gordon's theory of music acquisition, all of which are described below. Lorna's philosophy of teaching, as evidenced by the age divisions of the levels of curricula (see table 4), follows the concept of the gradual unfolding of children's readiness for learning.

According to McDonald and Simons, "Rousseau was himself a musician, and seemed to recognize 'appropriate' musical objectives for young children ... He advocated childlike songs for children; if none were available, teachers should create their own" so long as they are appropriate for a child's age and interests (McDonald and Simons 1989, 6). But Rousseau warned:

> I do not disapprove of nurses amusing the child with songs, and very cheerful and varied accents; but I do disapprove of her stunning him with a multitude of useless words of which he comprehends nothing except the tone she throws into them. (Rousseau 1893, 36, in McDonald and Simons 1989, 6)

Lorna's particular philosophy also recognizes that music for children should have lasting value. In Lorna's curricula, instrumental music is of the highest quality and includes classical as well as folk music of many cultures played with authentic instruments by professional musicians. Songs with words, even if translated into English, are traditional children's folk songs and fit within a five-note range, making them easily accessible for the child's developing vocal mechanism and transferrable to the keyboard when the child progresses into the keyboard curriculum. Songs for singing are in many tonalities and meters, but in general are limited to the range of D above middle C to A five notes above, as this is the healthiest range for young children's voices. Thus, children are exposed from the beginning to a wide variety of instrumental music and children's folk songs in a variety of tonalities and meters, but always using the highest quality of music.

Johann Heinrich Pestalozzi (1746–1827)

Pestalozzi established a school for orphans in 1796 (Keene 1982, 85) and in 1801 published *How Gertrude Teaches Her Children*, a guidebook for mothers to help them teach children too young to leave home (McDonald and Simons 1989, 6). Pestalozzi advocated that "experience should precede theory. Music learning, therefore, should begin with singing" (McDonald and Simons 1989, 6). His teachings and focus on music in education, especially his focus on *anschauung*, "or learning through the senses," attracted American educators Horace Mann and Lowell Mason (Keene 1982, 86, 87, 94). Therefore, "the earliest methods used in [American] public school music instruction thus were based on the logic of 'sound before sight' and 'practice before theory'; listening and singing experiences led to an understanding of notation and theory" (Campbell and Scott-Kassner 2002, 9).

Sound-before-sight is one of the foundational building blocks of the *Musikgarten* curricula, although it was not part of the *Curriculum Musikalische Früherziehung*. Gordon's *Music Learning Theory* (described below) is based upon sound-before-sight. Lorna learned of the sound-before-sight philosophy when she met Audrey and learned the principles of Montessori's teachings. The *Musikgarten* curricula, first published in 1994, are based upon the principle of experience-precedes-theory, or sound-before-sight.

Friedrich Froebel (1782–1852)

Froebel, a student of Pestalozzi, is known as "the founder of the kindergarten" and as "the educator who was to place [music] at the core of preschool education" (McDonald and Simons 1989, 7). Much of Froebel's early childhood was spent alone, becoming close to nature; his formal schooling began when he was ten, and he was not impressed with the lessons that seemed to have no connection to life experiences. He later expressed that education for the young should not be considered schooling but rather a time for children to "freely develop" (Puckett and Diffily 2004). His *Mother-Play and Nursery Songs* (1844/1878/1898)[13] "illustrates [his] romantic view of children as being one with nature" (Puckett and Diffily 2004). Froebel believed children learn not through formal teaching but through play and "experience, or 'self-activity' ... It is from playful activities that learning derives" (McDonald and Simons 1989, 7).

Review of the current and past *Musikgarten* curriculum documents indicates the prevalence of playful activities, including many fingerplay activities, which seem to have been an important part of Froebel's ideas, as his 1878 publication is entitled *Mother Play and Nursery Songs with Finger Plays* (Boston: Lothrop, Lee and Shepard Co.) (Puckett and Diffily 2004, 431).

Lorna's philosophy of teaching includes the importance of play as evidenced by the activities in the *Musikgarten* curriculum. She recognizes that children learn through movement and play; therefore, many of the songs that are repeated throughout the *Musikgarten* repertoire, from *Family Music for Babies* through *Music Makers: At the Keyboard*, are learned through movement and games. By the time children take the songs to the keyboard, the melodies are not only well loved but also well known to the point that transitioning them from the body to the fingers at the keyboard is easy and natural.

Fingerplay is an important component of the process of taking songs progressively through the *Musikgarten* curricula from *Babies* to *Keyboard*. Even though fingerplays are simple and fun for children, they benefit development. Fingerplays assist with fine motor and rhythmic development, as well as body awareness. "Knowing the body helps coordination which brings together thought, will and action," helping the child grow toward independence (Heyge and Sillick 1994/1997/2007, p 15). Coordination and fine motor skills are necessary for success at the keyboard. Additionally, Lillard (1996) pointed out that "in all

---

[13]   Three different dates are found for *Mother Play and Nursery Songs*.

this process, it is the hand operating with the brain that creates the child's intellect. Montessori called the hand 'the instrument of the intelligence'" (Lillard 1996, 27).

Twentieth-Century Early Childhood Development Theorists

Lorna considered the following six persons, each in his respective field, to be "great masters" in these three fields (Heyge 1999):

- Early childhood education
- Movement
- Music

Jean Piaget (1896–1980)

Swiss psychologist Jean Piaget was perhaps the twentieth century's most influential learning theorist. Piaget's "cognitive developmental theory" (Morrison 2004; Crain 2005) suggested approximate ages for a child's intellectual development. "Although the stages are commonly assigned a chronological range, Piaget was interested not so much in studying age-referenced characteristics as in interpreting developmentally sequenced characteristics" (Crain 2005, 24).

What had been important to Piaget was not the precise age of children, but that children's development followed a sequence of one period after another without missing one stage. Piaget's theory of cognitive development, as it applied to children from birth to age nine, had an influence upon the structure of the *Musikgarten* curriculum,[14] as illustrated here in table 1.

[14] Whether or not Piaget influenced Wucher for the *Curriculum Musikalische Früherziehung* is not known. Wucher indicated only that his program was well researched (Wucher 1996).

Table 1 *Piaget's General Periods of Development* (Crain, 2005, 115)

Period I	Sensorimotor Intelligence (birth to 2 years). Babies organize their physical action schemes, such as sucking, grasping, and hitting, for dealing with the immediate world.
Period II	Preoperational Thought (2 to 7 years). Children learn to think—to use symbols and internal images—but their thinking is unsystematic and illogical. It is very different from that of adults.
Period III	Concrete Operations (7 to 11 years). Children develop the capacity to think systematically, but only when they refer to concrete objects and activities.
Period IV	Formal Operations (11 to adulthood). Young people develop the capacity to think systematically on a purely abstract and hypothetical plane.

Musikgarten courses are divided by developmental age as suggested by Piaget and by Ed Gordon,[15] with consideration for physical and social development of children as well. For example, the sensorimotor stage of birth to two years of age is divided in the *Musikgarten* curricula into a course for babies before they become mobile and courses for toddlers who need more movement activities and space in which to move. The pre-operational stage is divided into courses for children ages three to four and then ages four to five, as well as ages five to six. Courses overlap according to both age and content in order to meet musical, as well as cognitive, developmental needs, depending upon whether or not children have progressed through the sequence of age-appropriate courses for a period of time or are just entering the sequence with no prior *Musikgarten* experience.[16] Other considerations for course development include a convenience factor for the family

---

[15] Gordon's theory will be considered later in the book.
[16] The current, complete offerings of the *Musikgarten* curricula appear as table 4.

that provides a range of activities suitable for a family group of parent/caregiver plus multiple children from birth to age five.[17]

In addition to the theory of the stages of development, Piaget also recognized that children experience a three-phase order to process new information: assimilation (taking in information), accommodation (making mental room for the new information), and equilibrium (restructuring thinking to include the new information) (Morrison 2004, 114–115).

The philosophy of teaching artistry espoused by Lorna and the teacher-trainers, described below, includes specific instruction that allows children to be guided by their own internal schedule of assimilation and accommodation rather than attempting to have all children learn at the same pace and process information in the same manner. Children will exhibit a variety of responses to new information and will participate in class, or not, in a variety of ways.

Table 2 *Piaget's Stages of Development and Musikgarten Curricular Considerations* (Adapted from Development of Musical Activities through Musikgarten, Musikgarten/Music Matters, Inc., Greensboro, NC; Piaget and Inhelder 2000; Crain 2005.)

Piaget's Stages	Characteristics	Musikgarten Curricula	Singing	Moving	Listening	Instrument Playing
Ages 0-2: Sensorimotor	Babies/toddlers look, hear, touch, grasp, and suck. There is no symbolic function or representation. First eight months are important to cognitive development. See *Notes	*Family Music for Babies* (babies prior to locomotion)	Singing is by adult caregiver. There is no expectation of singing from babies.	Bouncing and rocking by the caregiver are sensed by the baby. Babies begin to relate more rhythmically to music.	Music surrounds the baby (refer to Gordon's concept of the aural bath).	Instruments go into the mouth when the baby can grasp. By eight to ten months, purposeful rhythmic movement with instruments begins.

---

[17] *All Together Now* was specifically developed in 2006 in response to demand for multi-age offerings. Earlier *Family Music* courses also meet these multi-age needs with minor extensions of activities toward the younger or older children who might be attending.

Age/Stage	Cognitive Development	Product	Singing	Movement	Listening	Instruments
		Family Music for Toddlers /God's Children Sing I (older babies who are locomotive)	Singing is primarily by adult caregiver. Toddlers begin to join the singing when the music becomes very familiar.	Movement responses to music are likely. Begin high-energy locomotion--walking, running, start/stop, jumping.	Purposeful listening begins; e.g., recorded animal sounds. Child can attend to isolated thematic sounds.	Rhythm sticks, shakers, and drums can be rhythmically manipulated.
Ages 2-6: Preoperational Semiotic or Symbolic Function	The child begins to use symbolic thinking rather than needing sensory or tactile information. Thinking is not done with adult logic. Thinking is through child's perspective, not adult perspective. Child takes things literally.	*Cycle of Seasons/ God's Children Sing II* Children ages 3-4	Familiar songs are now sung by children. They become aware of tonality and are able to sing the "resting tone."	Impulse control, spatial awareness, and balance are all improved. Can participate in simple dances.	Contrasting sounds from nature (blue jay vs. cardinal) as well as instruments (oboe vs. clarinet) can be discerned.	Simple ostinati (steady instrumental pulses) can be played, especially with familiar songs.
		Music Makers At Home in the World/ Music Makers Around the World Children ages 4-6	Singing becomes more tuneful. Range and repertoire expand.	Movements and dances of specific cultures are explored.	Instrumental ensembles and compositions of specific cultures and styles are explored.	Two or more ostinati are explored simultaneously. Children enjoy ensemble opportunities.
Ages 7-11 Concrete Operations	The child becomes more successful in thinking logically and systematically; can deal with concrete objects. Child can see things from the perspective of others.	*Music Makers at the Keyboard* Children ages 7-9	Singing functions to internalize the material to be played at the keyboard.	Movement and dances are to foster ensemble skills, comprehension of meter, and familiarity of the songs.	Keyboard activities and homework include listening activities to promote skills necessary to play repertoire on the keyboard.	The keyboard is the primary instrument although resonator bars, drums, and other rhythm instruments are also utilized.

***Notes:** 1. Musikgarten does not utilize Piaget's six substages of the sensorimotor stage. 2. During the first eight months of life, "the child constructs all the cognitive substructures that will serve as a point of departure for his later perceptive and intellectual development, as well as a certain number of elementary affective reactions that will partly determine his subsequent affectivity" (Piaget and Inhelder 2000).

Maria Montessori (1870–1952)

Montessori's initial professional work as Italy's first female physician was to study institutionalized mentally retarded children (Standing 1957/1998, 28). Montessori developed a successful approach to teach reading and writing to these children. She later used this knowledge to teach in the Casa dei Bambini, a school she founded in 1907 for "over 50 extremely poor children—the sons and daughters of unemployed laborers, beggars, prostitutes, and criminals" (Crain 2005, 66). Montessori's ideas were not widely adopted in the United States until the launch of Sputnik in 1957, which caused Americans to become concerned about education and caused Montessori's work to come to "the attention of psychologists, educators, and the general public" (Gettman 1987; Kramer 1976 and Lillard 1972 in Crain 2005, 67).

Lorna encountered Montessori's philosophy in Toronto after she began teaching Kindermusik classes at the request of an organ-performance colleague; the classes drew the attention of Helma Trass, the principal of the Toronto Montessori School. For twelve years thereafter, Lorna worked successfully in the Montessori school as a music teacher. She developed a professional relationship with Audrey Sillick, who became a co-author of the *Kindermusik* and subsequent *Musikgarten* curricula (Heyge 2011a; L. Heyge, personal communication, May 7, 2011).

Montessori Teachings Apparent in Musikgarten Curricula

Each teacher's guide for the *Musikgarten* curricula contains a section on child development. The basic child-development material shows direct evidence of Montessori's influence through Lorna's working in the Montessori environment for twelve years and through her partnership with Audrey Sillick, Founder and Director Emeritus of the Toronto Montessori Teacher Training Institute, for the purpose of writing the curricula. The following list is not exhaustive but illustrates the inclusion of Montessori's teachings in the *Musikgarten* curricula.

- Children have an innate sense of what they need developmentally. Montessori admonished the teacher to follow the child. (Heyge and Sillick 1996/2003, 7; Sillick 1995, 23)
- A child's work is to self-construct into a unique person. (Heyge and Sillick 1996/2003 p.8; Sillick 1995, p. 23)
- Children need and seek order. (Lillard 1996, 11; Heyge and Sillick 1996/2003, 10)
- There are "two phases of development: 1) from birth to age three are years of intense activity and absorption; and 2) from three to six years is a time to consolidate the gains of the first period" (coordinating with unconscious/conscious absorbent mind). (Lillard 1996, 16; Heyge and Sillick 1996/2003 8; Sillick 1995, 24–25).
- "It is the hand operating with the brain that creates the child's intellect." (Montessori in Lillard 1996, 27; Heyge and Sillick 1994/1997/2007, 15)
- Children experience "critical periods" (coordinates with "sensitive periods") when children are focused on particular "work of inner construction." (Lillard 1996, 5; Heyge and Sillick 1996/2003, 8)
- "Sensorimotor exploration, order, movement, language and independence" are "identified for this age group." (Heyge and Sillick 1996/2003, 8; Lillard 1996, 11)
- Movement is critical for children, both for their mastery of their bodies and because they learn through movement. (Swan in Gettman 1987, xi; Heyge and Sillick 1996/2003, 8)
- Manipulatives used throughout the graded curricula are simple. For the youngest children, square nylon scarves, wooden rattles, rhythm sticks, and hand drums are the only manipulatives used (jingle sticks are not used in class until babies are of the age to no longer put the jingle in the mouth).
- For children three and up, picture cards (Lillard 1996, 30) are added (animals and birds to identify with recorded voices).
- The *Music Makers* series for children four and up uses developmentally appropriate pre-notation and notation

card games, advancing to printed notation song pages for the *Music Makers* curriculum once the sound-before-sight learning has been mastered successfully.

- Manipulatives and instruments should be in child-sensitive sizes, materials, and colors.
- There should be ceremonial aspects of obtaining and putting away instruments, folding scarves, or gathering children for special listening activities.
- Children learn about their world through their senses. *Musikgarten* provides ample tactile/sensory activities for all levels of development, from babies through older children.
- Children unfold developmentally. (Lillard /Heyge and Sillick)
- The child's first teacher is the parent. (Lillard/Heyge and Sillick 1996/2003, 7)
- Young children seem rested and satisfied at the completion of tasks that fit their developmental age ("sensitive periods"). (Lillard 1996, 25–26; Heyge and Sillick 1996/2003, 12)
- Children should do for themselves. (Lillard 1996, 29; Heyge and Sillick 1994/1997/2007, 9)

Twentieth-Century Movement Theorists

Émile Jaques-Dalcroze (1865–1950)

Dalcroze believed that "the most potent element in music and the nearest related to life is rhythmic movement" (Dalcroze 1921 in McDonald and Simons 1989, 150). Dalcroze noted that his "students were demonstrating mechanical, not musical, understanding" (Campbell and Scott-Kassner 2002, 72). He believed that "one of the functions of education should be to develop the musical instinct of children" (Dalcroze 1921 in McDonald and Simons 1989, 145–146). Dalcroze developed a system he called Eurythmics, which uses the body. He believed the body was "the first musical instrument on which we express our perceptions. Therefore, instruction using this instrument should precede all others" (McDonald and Simons 1989, 145). Dalcroze wanted "to enable children to perceive, express, and develop understanding of all the elements of music—melody, rhythm, dynamics, harmony, form, and style—through physical movement" (McDonald and Simons 1989, 145).

Dalcroze, a music educator, began with music as the basis of his teachings, adding movement to the music. For Lorna, the order of music first, then movement, was the appeal of Dalcroze (L. Heyge, personal communication, March 13, 2012). "Using music with movement creates experiential learning using the entire body, with steady beat, to teach the concepts of music through the musical movement" (A. Rucker, personal communication, March 13, 2012). For example, to sense the concept of legato, children visualize fish (and select which type of fish they want to imitate) and move freely around the room to Saint-Saëns' "Aquarium" from *Carnival of the Animals*.[18]

Rudolf Laban (1879–1958)

Laban devised a system of notation for ballet as well as a science of motion (Nash 1974). When used in work with children, Laban's movement theories are part of both locomotor and non-locomotor activities to increase body awareness (Cole 2000). Movement activities are "essential to the child's growth ... finding out how he moves, what he moves and where he moves ... to find out about his relationship to the environment, to develop spatial awareness, ease and grace, economy of motion" (Nash 1974).

Laban, a dancer, began with movement and with his ideas of weight, space, time, and flow; he added music to the movement (L. Heyge, personal communication, March 13, 2012). The feature of Lorna's classroom activity using Laban's theory, then,

---

[18] *Carnival of the Animals* is one of many classical and folk music pieces used throughout the *Musikgarten* curricula. The only music that is exclusively composed for the curricula is specifically for movement pieces requiring imaginative thought and purposeful movement. Otherwise, all music is classical from the standard repertoire of composers and periods, or folk music from many world cultures, authentically performed by ensembles with instruments of that culture. Dances are adapted from culturally appropriate folk dances using authentic musical accompaniment.

is the purposeful movement that explores weight, space, time, and flow (L. Heyge, personal communication, March 13, 2012). For example, to give children a sense of weight, space, time, and flow using Laban's techniques, children move to recorded music, pretending and sensing they are taking big steps through a snow pile or jumping into a puddle of water (A. Rucker, personal communication, March 13, 2012).

Twentieth-Century Music Theorists

Lorna recognized that both Orff and Kodály had influenced music education in Germany by the time she began teaching in the German music school system in 1971 (L. Heyge, personal communication, May 7, 2011).

Carl Orff (1895–1982)

The percussion instruments and music education curriculum of the Orff *Schulwerk*, derived by Gunild Keetman and Carl Orff between 1950 and 1954, are widely accepted today for classroom use in elementary schools worldwide. The basic principles of the method lend themselves well to early childhood programs, especially the principle that "music, dance and speech complement each other and at the same time provide starting points for creative activities" (Maubach 2006).

For Lorna, the influence of Orff is not only the particular instruments and their use but also ensemble work as suggested in the Schulwerk (A. Rucker, personal communication, March 13, 2012). Preparation for ensemble work begins early in the *Musikgarten* curricula as babies and toddlers explore rhythm instruments and three- to four-year-old children experience start-and-stop activities with the instruments. For example, several children play the shakers when the music indicates a soft sound, and the rest play the sticks when the rhythm changes and becomes lively. Ensemble work progresses appropriately according to age and skill level of the children, becoming more fully developed in the curriculum for ages six and up.

Zoltán Kodály (1882–1967)

Kodály had a passion for preserving the folk music and literature of Hungary. Kodály became concerned about the quality of music in the schools of Hungary and became an advocate of early childhood music (Lineburgh 2000, 22–23). In an interview in 1966, when asked about the age he thought music education should begin, the interviewer reported: "20 years ago he had said, 'The music education of the child should begin nine months before his birth,' but now when asked he says, 'It should begin nine months before the birth of the mother'" (Ernö 1966 in Lineburgh 2000, 22).

Kodály developed a "very careful, systematic approach to learning" (L. Heyge, personal communication, March 13, 2012). From Kodály's work, Lorna has adopted the use of movable-do *solfège* prior to sight reading, the sequence of teaching music to young children, and the "importance of listening, singing, and moving before notation" is read (A. Rucker, personal communication, March 13, 2012).

Contemporary Influences on Heyge's Philosophy

Audrey Sillick (1921–2014)

Audrey was born in India in 1921, was formally educated in England and Switzerland, and attended a teachers' college in India that was "totally committed to the education of young people" (Heyge 1999b). As a young child in India, Audrey spent much time outdoors, living "close to the animal and plant kingdoms, often playing in a garden filled with exotic fruits. Drama and story, nature and movement were a vital part of her childhood" (Heyge 1999b). Audrey met Maria Montessori while Montessori lived in India during World War II. At the time, Audrey could not foresee herself becoming a Montessori teacher, which she indeed did in the 1960s. She went on to found and to direct the Toronto Montessori Teacher Training Institute in 1971.

Audrey's early love of nature, story, and movement, coupled with her teacher-training in India and as a Montessori educator, helped create in her the rich educational vision that Lorna recognized when they became acquainted (Heyge 2011). In speaking of the integration of these aspects, Lorna said, "Audrey ... brings all of that in; and I'm the music person who's tempering it and finding the literature that goes with it. It's a wonderful development" (L. Heyge, personal communication, May 7, 2011).

As the diagnoses of autism and ADHD become more common, nature-deficit disorder is becoming recognized as a reality. Because of the integration of Audrey's nature-and-environment influence into Lorna's philosophy, the *Musikgarten* curriculum as a whole already addresses the issue:

> It turned out to be, as we move on and there are more and more learning disabilities recognized, more nature-deficit disorder recognized, and all of that, that I as an author—that our trainers as teacher-trainers—that our teachers have been sensitized for many years, but more specifically since 1994 with the first Musikgarten publication, to all of this. It's so much a part of Musikgarten, and it's a vital part of Musikgarten. It has everything to do with autism, with ADHD, with all of that—the work of Richard Louv[19] says it very nicely—you know, in a popular kind of a way. However, it's going to be brought to attention—and I think that's another enormous strength of what has come together under this name Musikgarten. (L. Heyge, personal communication, May 7, 2011)

Lorna attended Audrey's lectures on the varied aspects of child development and related the teachings to musical development. "Her lectures were very meaningful to me from the outset; and although ... having nothing to do with music development, I could listen to her words and hear them in relationship [to music]" (L. Heyge, personal communication, May 7, 2011).

---

[19]   Richard Louv is the author of *The Last Child in the Woods: Saving our Children from Nature-Deficit Disorder* (2006) and *The Nature Principle: Human Restoration and the End of Nature-Deficit Disorder* (2011), as well as other books. http://richardlouv.com/books/

Audrey Sillick, Founder (in 1971) and Director Emeritus of the Toronto Montessori Teacher Training Institute,[20] met Lorna in Toronto in 1980 and had a major influence on Lorna's work, becoming co-author with Lorna of all curricula from 1988 forward. Of their working relationship, Lorna said, "She and I together have shaped the entire body of [Musikgarten] work, all following the principles of holistic education which guide us professionally and personally" (Heyge 1999). Audrey's Montessori background, love of nature and science, and the broad scope of her knowledge about children deepened Lorna's teaching philosophy (Heyge 1999b).

> So, we have the work of 1988. The group of teacher-trainers is growing. I think it's important to say that this is my work; I'm the author and my name is on it. But it's a collective work—everybody, I hope, is influenced by what's going on. So this is an approach to teaching which continues to grow out of experiences and observations; and integrating more experiences. (L. Heyge, personal communication, May 7, 2011)

Audrey was a member of the Editorial Advisory Board of the *Early Childhood Connections* journal for the duration of its publication.[21] Lorna dedicated the summer 1999 issue, *Nature in Children's Lives,* to Audrey. In the editorial introduction to that issue, Lorna described Audrey as:

> ...mentor, elder, and friend to a large community of early childhood music and movement teachers.

---

[20] Source: Editorial Advisory Board listing, inside front cover, all issues of *Early Childhood Connections* journal, 1995–2005.

[21] Audrey Sillick contributed three articles to the *Early Childhood Connections* journal and co-wrote a fourth with Heyge: "Observation: What, Why, and How" (Vol. 1, No. 1); "Montessori's Gift: One Teacher's Point of View" (Vol. 1, No. 3); "Music: A Natural Way to Play with Babies" (with Heyge, Vol. 4, No. 4); and "Children at Home in the World: A Sense of Connection" (Vol. 5, No. 3). The summer 1999 issue (Vol. 5, No. 3), *Nature in Children's Lives,* was dedicated by Heyge to Sillick.

> Audrey has widened our horizons and brought us to a deeper understanding of holistic education. Through her thought and work, we participate in a view of life that understands our planet as a global village, interrelated biologically, psychologically, and socially. Hers is a dynamic vision which reveals that all levels of life, from molecular to mental, are interconnected and interdependent. (Heyge 1999b)

Lorna further stated that "with Audrey's guidance we travel the road to a holistic and integrated approach to music education" (Heyge 1999b).

> It was in 1984 that Audrey first addressed an international meeting of early childhood music and movement teachers about the nature of young children. From that beginning she has led us to honor and respect the abilities of children, to understand their movement and language needs, and to treasure nature as the outer world which feeds the inner world with beauty and wonder, two basic needs of humankind. (Heyge 1999b)

An important component to the idea of holistic education of the child is observation, very much a Montessori component as well as important to Audrey's love of nature. Lorna said that while observation was important in the German teaching, it became a stronger emphasis with Audrey's influence.

> It's becoming the observer, becoming the one who is open to "the environment" but the environment in its totality. And that's part of being a good teacher because you're taking in everything that's happening around you. And that's part of being holistic. Because we can't do anything without being in a place—and the place that children love to be is the world of nature. And how wonderful that this has been for us. (Heyge 2011)

Dee Joy Coulter

Dee Coulter is a neuroscience educator with a master's degree in special education from the University of Michigan and a doctorate in neurological studies and holistic education from the University of Northern Colorado. Dee suggested that early childhood music teachers "need to realize what music has to offer the mind" (Coulter 1995).

> There used to be a rich subculture of childhood— filled with songs, movement, and musical games— which was passed on from older to younger children in neighborhoods, on playgrounds, and within large families. Remarkably, we didn't realize the importance of these activities until they began to vanish. These activities were brilliant neurological exercises which introduced children to critical motor strategies, sensory tasks, and speech patterns in a playful context. Such activities were fun to practice until they were mastered. Children were naturally drawn to the development tasks they needed—once they were ready to learn them. So, what looked to us like 'child's play' was actually the serious work of preparing the body to learn. But times have changed. These playful workouts are dying out in many parts of the country. Kindergarten and first grade have become much more academic— rhythm bands, nursery rhymes and finger songs, rote learning chants, show and tell, and the conversational format of free play are gone ... Fortunately, more and more preschool age children are becoming beneficiaries of music and movement programs, thanks to the pioneering work of the advisors and editors of this journal and others. (Coulter 1995)

Dee was directly involved in the creation of the *Early Childhood Connections* journal in 1994 (Heyge 1995) and remained on the Editorial Advisory Board throughout the duration of its publication.

Dee contributed articles to the *Early Childhood Connections* journal to explain in layman's terms the neurological benefits of music.[22] She contributed to the material in the teacher's guides at all levels of the *Musikgarten* curricula, informing teachers of the most up-to-date research at the time of the writing of the guide. Because of the narrative design of the guides, Dee's contributions are seamless within the material. The following is an example of the combining of Dee's neurological contributions with Montessori's developmental contributions:

> At birth, the infant is plunged into a strange new world of bewildering sensations and impressions. At first, there is no distinction between self and not self. The infant has no memory, no language except a cry, and only reflexive, involuntary movement. The infant's work is to build two worlds—the world without and the world within. Out of the incredible barrage of sensations, infants create order in their world, forming a comprehensive, meaningful interrelated whole.
>
> This period of creative activity, of formation and metamorphosis, constitutes the child's work from birth to age 3. Through a series of critical periods, the infant learns to focus and assimilate various aspects of the environment in a particularly intense manner. It takes a unique mind to do this work, one which has no sense of self but is guided to develop by the pull of Nature's wisdom. (Heyge and Sillick 1997, 11)

---

[22] Dee Coulter's contributions to the journal were: "Music and the Making of Mind" (Vol. 1, No. 1); "Defending the Magic: Current Issues in Early Childhood Education" (Vol. 2, No. 2); and "Mind and Music in the 21st Century" (Vol. 6, No. 1). Coulter published a booklet in 1994, *Brain's Timetable for Developing Musical Skills*, and a CD set, *Mind and Music: Insights from Brain Science*, comprised of recordings of talks she gave at the National Early Childhood Music Conference, the Orff Schulwerk National Conference, the Kansas Music Teachers Association Conference, and the Fort Hays State University music conference.

In her article "Music and the Making of Mind" (Coulter 1995), Dee said that "music contributes to the academic journey of young students" (22) and that music teachers already and perhaps unknowingly teach what she called "thinking skills" to young children. Dee believes that, if music teachers were aware of the "value of [their] offerings," having that knowledge would increase the "potency" of the offerings (22). She suggested that with the "overly accelerated curriculum" elementary students now face (23), early childhood music activities can keep "a valuable part of childhood and a critical set of 'thinking skills' alive ... Music classes have helped ... children organize their body movements and their attention and have helped them develop the self-discipline needed in the academic classroom" (23). Such music activities as *London Bridge* or playing a barred percussion instrument (23), "nearly all work with musical instruments, most musical finger games, and clapping songs" (24), "standing, marching, keeping a beat, and moving rhythmically while they speak or sing" (24), standing up, "breath[ing] deeply, [changing] postures, and [moving] rhythmically" (25) are all neurologically beneficial to the young child and are regular activities in the early childhood music and movement class. The development of inner speech is critical to the young child's development: inner speech and impulse control are directly related and are aided by musical activities (25). When children are able "to internalize a sense of beat ... they will be able to hold their concentration for long periods of time without having to seek external metronomes like tapping, chewing, rocking, and humming" (26). The development of reasoning abilities is another benefit of the acquisition of inner speech and impulse control (26). Dee ended the article by telling the early childhood music educator: "You are, indeed, a vital contributor to the child's educational development" (26).

Lorna commissioned Dee to produce a publication for parents entitled *The Neuroscience of Music*. The three-set publication contains four separate monographs, each monograph addressing one aspect of music's neurological benefits.

> They're ten-minute talks. You're not going to read very much, but you're going to read it over and over;

and every sentence you can read and contemplate for a while. Some of it is at a social-enculturation level, some is on a more personal level; and some of it is how development manifests at different levels—for instance for the toddler and for the young child—plus what is the neurology behind each of these things. (Coulter, personal communication, August 9, 2010)

The three divisions of the publication address behavior, school skills, and creativity. The divisions and subdivisions, demonstrating music's neurological benefits, are as follows:

1. Behavior
   a. To relax and be calm
   b. To wait
   c. To control impulses
   d. To move with rhythm and grace

2. School skills
   a. To share, take turns, and speak up
   b. To sit still and listen
   c. To enjoy practicing
   d. To get ready to read

3. Creativity
   a. To fall in love with music
   b. To compose
   c. To improvise
   d. To love nature

All together, the three-division set of monographs provides neurological information in layman's language appropriate for parents and teachers to gain knowledge of music's benefits in each of these aspects of a young child's life.[23]

---

[23] *The Neuroscience of Music* is available from Musikgarten, 507 Arlington Street, Greensboro, NC.

Combined influence of Sillick and Coulter

Lorna addressed the combined influences of Audrey and Dee to her particular philosophy of teaching:

> So the influences on me or my work are the Audrey influences which brought in the Montessori and the world of nature; ... but it was, I would say, just in a very different way, a feeling-based world. You come to Dee and she brings in the neurological thinking and will throw in the research base for this and then bring it back around to the feeling of the child. So they're different influences— they're just very different influences. They both broaden the spectrum of how you see your work a great deal—a wonderful combination. (L. Heyge, personal communication, May, 7, 2011)

Edwin E. Gordon (b. 1927)

Gordon is a musician, researcher, and author whose "primary interests are research in the psychology of music, music aptitudes, music learning theory, audiation, and improvisation" (Gordon, 2004). Gordon was a member of the Editorial Advisory Board of the *Early Childhood Connections* journal for the duration of its publication.

Gordon's work can be briefly described as the theory that children learn music in the same way they learn language. Children are bathed in language in the womb and as infants long before they are expected to read and write. Music learning is most efficient and enjoyable for children when they follow the same developmental steps to music acquisition that they follow for language acquisition.[24] Gordon's system uses patterns of pitches—following the familiar *do-re-mi-fa-sol* scale in prescribed two- and three-pitch patterns—and of rhythms—again in short combinations of rhythms, using a language of Gordon's invention.

---

[24] Following Lorna's philosophy of holistic education, *Musikgarten's Pathway to Literacy* is her curricular plan that follows the natural developmental stages of both music and language literacy.

The idea of patterns in music follows the idea of combinations of letters in language that make up words or parts of words that are commonly found in language. Musikgarten incorporates the Gordon pattern system as well as his developmental-stage theory of children's readiness for each level of learning (see table 3).[25]

Lorna was introduced to Gordon's work through Joyce Jordan-DeCarbo at the University of Miami in 1986, and by 1994, Lorna had begun to adapt Gordon's rhythm and tonal patterns in her teaching; they remain an important part of each level of the curriculum (Heyge 2011). Table 3 illustrates Gordon's skill sequence and the basic *Musikgarten* curricular offerings.

---

[25] For a thorough but simplified explanation of Gordon's theory, see *The Ways Children Learn Music*, Eric Bluestine, 1995, GIA Publications, Chicago.

Table 3 *Gordon's Levels in the Musikgarten Curricula*
Adapted from Development of Musical Activities through Musikgarten, ©Musikgarten/Music Matters, Inc., Greensboro, NC

Gordon's MLT level	Musikgarten Curricula	Characteristic
Aural	*Family Music for Babies*	Being surrounded by music (aural bath); feeling rhythm through rocking and movement while held; sensory exploration of instruments.
Aural/Oral	*Family Music for Toddlers/ God's Children Sing I*	Continuing as above but now able to respond by themselves; begin own movement to rhythms; begin to echo patterns.
Verbal Association/ Partial Synthesis	*Cycle of Seasons/ God's Children Sing II*	Able to sing with pitch and rhythm; has impulse control and spatial awareness; purposefully moves to music; can distinguish sounds; transfers movement ideas to instruments.
Verbal Association/ Partial Synthesis/ Symbolic Association	*Music Makers: At Home*	Sings more tunefully; explores Laban elements of weight, time, space, flow; more advanced discrimination of sounds in solo and ensemble; able to maintain *ostinati* (steady instrumental pulses); able to recognize familiar patterns in songs and notation.

Partial Synthesis/ Symbolic Association/ Composite Synthesis	*Musik Makers: Around the World*	Has expanded range and repertoire; can explore movement and dance; instrument ensembles possible; can now participate in ensemble with two or more ostinati; can visually recognize familiar patterns in written songs and can *audiate* (hear sound patterns in his or her head).
Symbolic Association/ Composite Synthesis/ Generalization/ Composition-Improvisation/ Theoretical Understanding	*Music Makers: At the Keyboard*	Sings to internalize material to be played on keyboard; comprehends meter; higher level dance and ensemble skills; transposes known songs to several keys; builds a repertoire of visually and aurally familiar patterns; applies knowledge for improvisation.

Principles of the Philosophy

It is important that a distinction be made between Lorna's published curricula, which comprise the most current and visible documented evidence of Lorna's unique pedagogical philosophy, and the philosophy itself. So a definition of "pedagogical philosophy" is appropriate at this time. The term as I use it is this: one's pedagogical philosophy is the compilation of knowledge, experiences, and attitudes into principles that govern one's teaching.

In that regard, I have identified four main principles that I believe are the most fundamental to Lorna's pedagogical philosophy. These are the four main principles of her teaching ideals that make her philosophy unique:

1. Holistic education
2. Teaching artistry
3. Parent and family involvement
4. Music for all children

In the interview for *Keyboard Companion*, Lorna listed many principles that guide her work (Johnson 2006, 35–37). However, the research for my dissertation led to the four main principles that are described below. The products of Lorna's philosophy are described later in this book.

Holistic Education

Lorna believes that when we teach, we teach the whole child, "addressing all the developmental areas of learning—aural, visual, motor, socio-emotional and language" (Jordan-DeCarbo, personal communication, April 12, 2011). Robin Britt said Lorna's curriculum, which follows her philosophy, addresses all the domains of school readiness, a subject with which he is familiar because of his work with Smart Start, Project Uplift, and Head Start centers in North Carolina (R. Britt, personal communication, May 26, 2011).

The word *holistic* appears repeatedly in interviews with Lorna (Heyge 2011; Hannagan 2010; Johnson 2006) and documents written by Lorna (Heyge 1995b, 2002, 2011; Heyge and Sillick 1998, 1997; Heyge, Hannagan, and Wilson 2001).

Lorna used the word in several ways:

- when considering the entire environment of a child's world
- when considering the entire approach to music education
- when considering the education of the child in all domains of learning as well as using the entire body for learning (Heyge 2011).

Lorna stated that she "follow(s) the principles of holistic education" (Heyge 1999). She defined those principles in two parts:

1. referring specifically to music education
2. referring broadly to general education of the whole child

Holistic approach to music education

> Looking back [at the work of the Association of German Music Schools], holistic education was always emphasized from a music-holistic point of view. If you think about it, most experiences for young children are beginning instrumental lessons. And the Germans were saying—right back at the beginning—no, that's not the foundation for music education. We need to be doing singing, we need to be doing movement, we need to be doing chanting, we need to be doing listening; and I think they were really absolutely on the cutting edge with the listening program they developed at the time. So they were talking about a holistic ... let's say a broad-based program musically—it was, right from the beginning. That was what was attractive about it to me ... that was what made it work ... So, from a holistic point of view, that word applied to the approach to music. (L. Heyge, personal communication, May 7, 2011)

Education of the whole child

An important aspect of the uniqueness of Lorna's particular philosophy is her bringing together information from fields related to early childhood music, especially from the works of Audrey and Dee. For example, Lorna attended Audrey's lectures at the Montessori Teacher Training Institute; and she began making connections between music and child psychology, neurology, and language development. She sensed that "our own field of the music side of teaching needs so much influence from these other fields ... [a] holistic approach—[an] integrated approach" (Heyge 2011). Through her association with Audrey's teachings, Lorna developed an understanding of holistic education.

> Only from a holistic viewpoint can the whole person of the child—body, mind, and spirit—be considered. The psychosomatic unity of the child is a dynamic factor in the process of learning and requires the engagement of the whole person. (Sillick 1995, 23–24)

Teaching Artistry

The type of research I conducted for the dissertation from which this book is adapted is called qualitative research. It is research based on ideas and words rather than on an experiment and numbers. Experiment-and-numbers research is known as quantitative research. The rules for qualitative research allow for information to emerge—to grow out of the work as it is being done. (In quantitative research, basically, the focus of the research has to be specified from the start.) While *teaching artistry* was not a topic I initially expected to hear about, during our conversation Lorna spoke of teaching artistry as an important quality—a quality that, to my mind, is the heart and soul of Lorna's gift and of her philosophy.

Lorna cautioned that the concept she called teaching artistry is difficult to grasp. She said, "I don't know how you say that on paper" (L. Heyge, personal communication, May 7, 2011).

Lorna spoke of this artistry as being a synthesis of music education, child development education, neurological education, language education, and psychological education—truly a synthesis of everything her philosophy encompasses—the depth and richness that makes *Musikgarten* truly the song from her heart. "I don't think you can be a good teacher of young children without this" (L. Heyge, personal communication, May 7, 2011).

To Lorna, the important contribution that Musikgarten makes "both on the curricular side and on the teacher-training side" (L. Heyge, personal communication, May 7, 2011) is this synthesis. Lorna's carefully developed synthesis of musical, environmental, developmental, and psychological factors is what created her particular philosophy of teaching, which uniquely contributed to the field of early childhood music and movement, if not to early childhood education in general.

To Lorna, the teaching artistry that she values so highly in her work, and rightly so, is not something that a music student can learn from books in a college classroom environment. Lorna's teaching artistry is a core principle of her philosophy—perhaps the most important principle—and is passed down in the *Musikgarten* tradition (as it was in the original *Kindermusik* tradition) from Lorna to her teacher-trainers to the Musikgarten teachers in the field. In Lorna's own words:

> And so that is a contribution which Musikgarten makes—both on the curricular side, but probably equally important on the teacher-trainer workshop side—because if it were only in the books, it still wouldn't be reaching the people. (L. Heyge, personal communication, May 7, 2011)

Lorna spoke of the importance of the personal attention to teaching—to transmitting what is important through personally training her teacher-trainers and through their personally training all new teachers in the Musikgarten philosophy:

> One of the great pleasures for me is to see as we do in the Foundation work [training Head Start teachers in the Music for Learning program], with [the teachers being trained] almost without knowing they're doing it, pick up teaching skills; and those teaching skills aren't … playing 16th notes better; they are part of this whole person and their approach to teaching … It's being around this

whole attitude towards teaching and children and integrated learning. (Heyge 2011)

Working closely with Audrey from 1980 onward, Lorna refined her teaching philosophy as well as her personal teaching artistry in the Montessori environment. According to Audrey:

> Anyone involved in this kind of work is in a sense an artist. You pull into it, you practice it, you see how it goes. You have to get the essence of the thing and know it. Having done that, and having done everything just right, you dare to improvise. The improvisation is not guided by some pattern you have in your head but by the children you are teaching. (Sillick 1995)

Lorna spoke of the combination of the influences of Audrey and Dee upon her, of her pulling together those influences and melding them into her work, and of passing that on to the teacher-trainers, who then give back to Lorna their unique experiences of working with the curriculum itself, as well as their experiences of teaching, thus creating a cycle of teaching philosophies, knowledge, and experience that enriches the complete work. Lorna stressed the fact that although this is her work with her name on it, it is very much the work of many. The cycle of experience, transmission, and sharing is what solidifies the complete pedagogical philosophy that is passed on by the artistry of teaching from Lorna to the teacher-trainers to new Musikgarten teachers. And it is this critical, central philosophy that allows Musikgarten teachers to effectively engage in teaching much more than nice music lessons. It is this central philosophy that allows Musikgarten classrooms to be special places where holistic education is taking place---where the whole child is considered and nourished.

> There's so much that infuses the teaching that you can't really write down in a book. That, I know, has been passed in part successfully through me to the group of teacher-trainers. Yes; and their influence

is on me, too, because that is the enormous richness
that we have—we come together every year, they
watched me teach, have been trained by me ...
they go out and have their experiences, come back
and it's shared and further developed. (L. Heyge,
personal communication, May 7, 2011)

Lorna's teaching artistry has greatly influenced Musikgarten
Executive Vice President Jill Hannagan's teaching. Hannagan
recognized the influence of Audrey and Dee upon Lorna's
philosophy when she said, "It was just their way of being with
children, and it's about much more than the curriculum itself" (J.
Hannagan, personal communication, June 27, 2011).

Parent and Family Involvement

Parent and family involvement, both by the parent attending
the class with the child and the parent and family participating
at home with the child, is an important component of Lorna's
philosophy. In speaking of the beginnings of her work in Germany,
Lorna said that "the parents were involved—they were part of the
class at the end [of each class], [and] the communication was quite
good right from the beginning" (Heyge 2011).

Lorna strongly advocates family involvement in music making.
She said "music making belongs in the family ... The *time* to
start experiencing music is in early childhood; the *place* is in the
family" (Heyge in Johnson 2006, 35). In planning the *Musikgarten*
curricula, Lorna focuses on keeping a balance according to the age-
related stages of development; and in each lesson, she concentrates
on how that balance of activities would be carried home by the
attending parent who would then have the week to make music
with the child.

What does a child need at birth? What does he
need emotionally? What does he need physically?
What does that have to do with music? What are
the music needs? What are the first responses? How

can we put *this* together with *this*? How can we then say—and this is so important—the child is with me for 30 minutes—he's with mother/caregiver/nanny/whoever for the rest of the week. How do I teach that child through the parent? So what do I have to adjust to hook the parents so that they take this home, which is where it's really going to happen? And all of those things are part- and-parcel of what we do. (L. Heyge, personal communication, May 7, 2011)

A component of the original *Kindermusik* program (1974–1994) was the *Parents' Pages* that went home after every lesson. These were first used by Wucher in the German curriculum and adapted by Lorna into *Kindermusik*. At all levels of the current *Musikgarten* curriculum, family home materials are available and encouraged, not only for the child's benefit of reinforcement of music activities covered in class but also to encourage family involvement during the week. Parents or caregivers are required to attend classes with children three years old and younger and are encouraged to attend the last fifteen minutes of class for the *Music Makers* sequential-curriculum series (ages five and up). Lorna strongly encourages Musikgarten teachers to hold informational parent meetings and to keep parents well informed about the philosophy and the importance of what is being taught in the classes.

> Parent Time is the special part of class when children and adults share the joy of group music-making ... During Parent Time, the companion adults learn aurally—the same way that their children are learning. This kind of learning must be experienced so that parents understand how they can aid their children (and oftentimes themselves) on the pathway to music literacy. (Heyge, Hannagan, and Wilson 2001)

Music for All Children

In American society, preschool music education is mainly taught by private teachers, and classes are attended by the "twice-blessed children, those whose parents seek music experiences for their children, and have sufficient income to pay for it" (Heyge in Johnson 2006). Lorna believes "we must strive to widen the circle of children who can benefit from music" (Heyge in Johnson 2006). For Lorna, extending the circle of children means including children from low-income families as well as children whose families can afford the private education. Therefore, for many years, Lorna volunteered in Head Start centers and believes strongly that music education positively influences children's school readiness.

> Since January, 1992, I have taught weekly in low-income, four-year-old classrooms. In my capacity as volunteer music teacher for these classes, I have attempted to strike a balance between the needs of children, the strengths of the community, and what I could contribute through my educational experiences. The benefits to these children are readily seen. In addition to the inherent joy which comes from making music, early childhood music education offers them the potential for significant language development, improvement of gross motor skills, refinement of fine motor skills, and social development—competencies particularly needed by low-income children. While all children need these competencies, children in Head Start settings seem to need more opportunities for developing these skills than do children in other settings. And, music-and movement-based experiences offer these children one of their best opportunities for acquiring such skills. (Heyge 2000)

Mr. Robin Britt, Executive Director of Guildford (NC) County Child Development, met Lorna in 1991 when Lorna volunteered to teach music at Britt's Project Uplift, a non-profit outreach program for low-income families. "Lorna has this intense sense of contributing to the community, and a very strong sense of identification with low-income families" (R. Britt, personal communication, May 26, 2011). Lorna taught Britt "the importance of music and movement as a means of developmental, and for that matter, cognitive, and physical, and all the domains of school readiness. Music has a very strong impact on that" (R. Britt, personal communication, May 27, 2011).

Products of the Philosophy

The Curriculum

Prior to entering the field of early childhood music education in 1971, Lorna taught organ and music classes to college-age students. When Lorna began to teach the *Curriculum Musikalische Früherziehung* program to the young children in Germany, she began to see solutions to musical problems of her college-level organ-performance students. Lorna found the solutions in the broad-based music literacy approach of Wucher's curriculum. The solutions, the basic building blocks of music taught to young children, made sense to her (Heyge in Johnson 2006; Heyge 2011b).

The original Kindermusik curriculum

During her 1973 translation process of the *Curriculum Musikalische Früherziehung*, Lorna began to substitute English-language songs and culturally relevant illustrations (L. Heyge, personal communication, May 7, 2011; L. Robinson, personal communication, June 6, 2011). In 1974, Wucher wanted the program tested in the United States; therefore, Lorna brought her English translation of the German curriculum, trademarked for

American use under the new name *Kindermusik*[26] (Heyge 1999). The first classes were taught at Greensboro College in Greensboro, North Carolina (L. Heyge, personal communication, May 7, 2011; Heyge, 1999). Still working with the English translation of the German curriculum, Lorna began training new teachers in 1975 (Hannagan 2010). Lorna related that "in the fall of 1974, I started to teach 72 children in 6 classes. Greensboro was a fruitful ground; and in January 1975, we started several new classes taught by 3 teachers from Greensboro whom I trained" (Heyge 1999).

The first English-language adaptation, released in 1979, was published by the German company Gustav Bosse Verlag Regensburg (Heyge 2011; *Kindermusik Music Primer* title page) distributed in the United States and Canada by Magna-Music Baton, St. Louis, Missouri.[27] This publication was the translation of the German work, but with English-language song literature (or translations of German songs into English) and culturally relevant illustrations.

---

[26] "Editor's note: The North American adaptation entitled *Kindermusik* was published in 1978 by the G. Bosse Publishing Co. (Regensburg/ Kassel) and was distributed initially by Magna-Music Baton (1978-1984) and thereafter by Music Resources International (1984-1988). Current products entitled *Kindermusik* are not related to the German curriculum. Rather, the North American adaptation of the *Curriculum Musikalische Früherziehung* is now available through the National Guild of Music Schools under the title *Tonekinder*." (Wucher, 1996)

[27] From *Kindermusik* curriculum, *Music Primer*. Copyright information inside the *Music Primer* indicates the following: This *Music Primer* is part of the Curriculum: *Kindermusik, Music for the Very Young*, the English adaptation of the Curriculum: *Musikalische Früherziehung* of the Association of German Music Schools. It has been prepared by a team of authors from the Association of German Music Schools: Diethard Wucher, chairman, with assistance in particular from Irmgard Benzing, Heidi Geck, Siegfried Fink, Peter Heilbut, Rainer Mehlig, Günther Noll and Lucie Steiner. This Curriculum is a new edition of the Program *Musikalische Früherziehung* of the Association of German Music Schools, published by Diethard Wucher and Wilhelm Twittenhoff. English version adapted by Lorna Lutz Heyge. Rights of melodies and words: The songs of 27b, 29b, 34b are traditional. All other melodies and words are protected by Gustav Bosse Verlag, Regensburg, W. Germany.

Lorna separated from the German publisher in 1985 and established Music Resources International "to distribute the *Kindermusik* curriculum" (Hannagan 2010), which it did until 1994, when Lorna established Musikgarten/Music Matters, Inc. Music Matters continues to publish the *Musikgarten* materials (Heyge 2011).

Curriculum for two-year-old children

The *Curriculum Musikalische Früherziehung* as well as Lorna's original English-language adaptation, *Kindermusik* (1971–1994), was limited to two-year, sequential music education programs for four- to six-year-old children (Wucher 1996; Heyge 2011). In 1990, Lorna published a curriculum for two-year-old children under the publishing company Music Resources International.

Musikgarten: Expansion of course offerings

Since 1994, Musikgarten/Music Matters, Inc., has expanded the curriculum to include education for children from birth to age nine. The current curricular offerings and their publication dates are shown in table 4, below.

Table 4 *Musikgarten Curricula* (Source: Musikgarten/ Music Matters, Inc., updated June, 2015)

Year/ Revision(s)	Early Childhood Series		Lorna Heyge and Audrey Sillick, authors
1997/2007	*Family Music for Babies*	newborn to 18 months	
1996/2003	*Family Music for Toddlers*	15 months to 3-1/2 years	
1994/1999/2007	*The Cycle of Seasons*	3 to 5 years	
1995/2000/2010	*Music Makers–At Home in the World*	from age 4	
1997/2001/2015	*Music Makers– Around the World*	from age 6	

1995/2005	*God's Children Sing*	1-1/2 to 5 years	Cathy Mathia and Linda Robinson, co-authors
2009	*Music Keys* for preschool settings	age 4	Linda Robinson, author
	Keyboard Series		Lorna Heyge, Mary Louise Wilson, Jill Hannagan, co-authors
2009	*Introduction to the Keyboard*	from age 6	
2001	*Music Makers–At the Keyboard, Books 1 and 2*	ages 6 to 9	
2002/2007	*Music Makers–At the Keyboard, Books 3 and 4*		
2008	*Music Makers–At the Keyboard, Books 5 and 6*		
2007/2009	*Musikgarten Adults–Enjoying the Piano Together, Books 1–3*	16 and up	Lorna Heyge, Mary Louise Wilson, Jill Hannagan, Autumn Keller, co-authors
	Additional Programs	**birth through kindergarten**	
2000/2004	*My Musical World*		
1998/2007	*Nature's Music*		
2006	*Nimble and Quick; Twist and Turn: All Together Now— Family Music Series*		Lorna Heyge, Martha Hallquist, co-authors
1994/1999/2008	*The Cycle of Seasons--Summer*		

	Additional Programs	ages 4 to 7	
1997	*Nature Trail*		
2006	*Drumming and Dancing*		
2008	*Music Makers–At Home in the World*: *Seashore*		
2011	*Music Makers–At Home in the World*: *My Neighborhood Community*		

Keyboard curriculum

In 1999, Lorna, Mary Louise Wilson, and Jill Hannagan began work on a keyboard curriculum. In addition to each author having a strong keyboard background, Mary Louise has a doctorate in music education, Jill has a background in Gordon's *Music Learning Theory*, and Lorna has experience developing curriculum. According to Lorna, "We just got to the point where the time was right ... And it is through that period that Ed [Gordon]'s work ... became more and more developed [into our curriculum]" (Heyge 2011). Table 3 illustrates aspects of Gordon's *Music Learning Theory* and associated *Musikgarten* curricula.

The Kindermusik Teachers Association

Lorna formed the Kindermusik Teachers Association by holding the first meeting in 1984 "as the teachers kept expressing the desire [to come together] ... It's being together with other people—it's also an exchange about what we're doing ... The original idea ... was to learn more about teaching the children—to foster this community" (Heyge 2011).

The first meeting was informal; invitation was by a personally typed letter from Lorna. Beginning in 1986, a formal convention was held every two years through 1994. Since 1996, the meetings have been held by the Early Childhood Music Association/Early Childhood Music and Movement Association, as explained below.

In 1994, the Kindermusik Teachers Association board voted to change the name of the organization to the Early Childhood Music Association so that it reflected the field in general, rather than reflecting a specific curriculum, "in an attempt to be a forum for anyone teaching music to young children, regardless of what curriculum they were using" (Hannagan 2010). Later, in 1998,[28] the name was changed to Early Childhood Music and Movement Association in order to reflect the importance of movement in the early childhood curriculum (Heyge 2011). Lorna was directly responsible for the KTA, and therefore her pedagogical philosophy was the philosophy under which the member-teachers taught and by which the KTA was governed. Even though the ECMMA evolved directly from the KTA, the focus of the organization changed when the name was changed, and it is now an organization for all early childhood music and movement teachers. At the present time, any connection with Lorna's philosophy and the ECMMA is reflected "probably only through the participation of any of our Musikgarten people who are involved in it" (Heyge 2011).

Professional Journal—Early Childhood Connections

In her article "Commentary," which opened the first issue of the *Early Childhood Connections* journal, Lorna (1995) said:

> From across the broad spectrum of innovative early childhood educational approaches, *Early Childhood Connections* is bringing together definitive thinkers at the forefront of educational theory, research, and practice whose early childhood music and movement experiences are based on actual work with children.
>
> The idea for *Early Childhood Connections* was conceived in an impromptu telephone conversation with Dee Coulter in January 1994 and born during a meeting of music and movement educators in early

---

[28] [26] Date verified at http://www.ecmma.org/resources/history/

March ... With this first issue, dreams of gathering together an early childhood music and movement forum have become concrete ... Our invitation to every reader of *Connections* is this: let us use this forum to share our knowledge, to define what we have in common, to examine new viewpoints, and to clarify goals for the children in our care. Through dialogue and discussion, we will refine our points of view and put forth a clear vision which supports children, families, and our culture ...

We live in a time when individuals from vastly different fields are beginning to realize that we must work together in a new way. *Early Childhood Connections* aspires to helping establish this new path. This journal has been launched with a lofty goal: to provide a central voice for all who are concerned about and are interested in music and movement in early childhood education—from the practitioner/teacher to the researcher/academician, from the parent to the policy maker ... (Heyge 1995)

Lorna assembled a group of "celebrated board members who have readily agreed to support this journal in addition to their already busy and productive lives" (Heyge 1995). The Editorial Advisory Board consisted of the following:[29]

- Lois Birkenshaw—Course Director for Orff Program, Royal Conservatory of Music, Toronto; Author, Consultant, Authority for Children with Special Needs
- Robin Britt—Secretary of the Department of Human Resources, State of North Carolina
- Karl Bruhn—Arts Education Advocate
- Timothy Caldwell—Dalcroze Authority; Professor of Music, Central Michigan University

---

[29] *Early Childhood Connections*, Vol. 1, No. 1.

- Elizabeth B. Carlton—Assistant Professor of Music, Catawba College, North Carolina; Music Consultant and Author, High/Scope Educational Research Foundation
- Dee Joy Coulter, EdD—Neuroscience Educator, The Naropa Institute, Colorado; University of Northern Colorado
- William B. Davis, PhD—RMT Associate Professor of Music Therapy, Colorado State University
- John Feierabend, PhD—Professor, Director of Music Education Division, and Director of National Center for Music and Movement in the Early Years, The Hartt School, University of Hartford
- Edwin E. Gordon, PhD—Educator, Researcher, and Author in Music Learning Theory, Music Aptitudes, and Audiation
- Jane M. Healy, PhD—Learning Specialist, Author, Consultant, Lecturer
- Joyce Jordan-DeCarbo, PhD—*Early Childhood Connections* Research Review Editor; Associate Professor of Music Education, University of Miami
- Lilian G. Katz, PhD—Director of ERIC Clearinghouse on Elementary and Early Childhood Education, University of Illinois; President, National Association for the Education of Young Children
- Catherine Mathia—President, Early Childhood Music Association
- Grace C. Nash—Music Specialist, Orff Authority, Author
- Audrey Sillick—Founder and Director Emeritus, Toronto Montessori Teacher Training Institute
- Phyllis S. Weikart—Associate Professor Emeritus, University of Michigan; Movement Consultant and Author, High/Scope Educational Research Foundation

Lorna welcomed a variety of opinions to the journal and saw it as a venue for articles from all persons interested in the field of early childhood music education.

> From an editorial standpoint, our policy was to have different points of view, to keep it non-commercial, to solicit [contributions by] the main players—John

Feierabend wrote, Ken Gilmartin wrote, Phyllis
Weikart I think did, Ed Gordon obviously—
and so certainly not everything is mine ... but I
approved, maybe not the content of every article,
but certainly the summary of every article—and
Martha [Hallquist] and I were on one page as to
what the journal was supposed to be ... There are
authors that we wanted to invite to write whose
words I would not, if I were asked to, defend ... I
would say I don't agree with that—but I think it's
important they would be in that journal ... [The
journal reflected] my support of the development
of the field and the coming together of the field.
(Heyge 2011)

Foundation for Music-Based Learning

In 1993, Lorna and Hermann Heyge began the Foundation for
Music-Based Learning. From 1995 through 2005, the Foundation
published the *Early Childhood Connections* journal. In her closing
editorial of the journal, Lorna stated that the Foundation would
"continue using its assets exclusively for charitable purposes for the
betterment of children and families and will direct its resources
to research, teaching and the dissemination of knowledge" (Heyge
2005).

As of this writing, the Foundation supports Music for Learning,
administered by Linda Robinson, who joined Lorna in 1976 as a
Kindermusik teacher-trainer. Music for Learning is a two-year-
cycle program for four-year-old children taught by experienced
Musikgarten teachers in early childhood development centers,
such as Head Start, that serve low-income families. Its purpose
is twofold:

- To help enhance the children's school readiness through
  Musikgarten music instruction twice a week

- To train the classroom teacher and center director to provide the Musikgarten program to the children in the center

The Musikgarten teacher teaches the class of children for the first year and assists and observes the classroom teacher the second year. The Musikgarten teacher holds two family-music nights per year to involve the families and model the activity for the classroom teacher and director. The Musikgarten teacher also holds eight professional-development sessions per year to train the classroom teacher and the center director to continue the program in the classroom when the Musikgarten teacher completes the two-year commitment. Lorna spoke of personal experience teaching children in Head Start centers:

> Through the Foundation for Music-Based Learning, I have spent many years bringing music to various Head Start settings. I have seen success on three levels:
> 1. the teaching itself is a joy for all;
> 2. what we observe (qualitatively) is that the children make advances in motor, language and social skills;
> 3. what we measure (quantitatively) ... shows that a well-constructed, well-taught music and movement program has a significant affect [sic] on children's communication skills.
>
> Communication skills are directly related to language development and literacy—a critical concern for our children today. (Heyge in Johnson 2006)

CHAPTER SIX

SUMMARY

Lorna's Heyge's particular philosophy of teaching is informed by the historical theories of Comenius, Rousseau, Pestalozzi, and Froebel, who advocated for education of the very young child, as well as Jean Piaget's theories of the stages of development and three steps to information processing, plus the teachings of Maria Montessori. Contemporary influences include Audrey Sillick, Dee Coulter, and Ed Gordon. Lorna began her teaching career as an organ professor and musicologist. She began teaching young children when hired as an assistant director of the Troisdorf neighborhood music school in Germany in 1971.

As the researcher for the dissertation that became this book, I identified four major points of Lorna's philosophy, which are:

1. Holistic education
2. The artistry of teaching,
3. Parent and family involvement
4. Music for all children

The explanations given previously in this text for each of these four points highlight the core of Lorna Heyge's unique philosophy, but it is her teaching artistry that gives her work its life and breath. All four points of Lorna's philosophy are important, and many others besides these are woven together into the tapestry that we see. But her personal teaching artistry takes this tapestry and floods it with brilliant sound and color that is not found elsewhere.

I believe the words of Dee Coulter best summarize what is unique about Lorna Heyge's teaching philosophy and lifework:

> The curriculum is so sound, they were able to even have music-as-literacy training. So this particular program can teach language competencies or impulse control or socialization. It has integrity to its design, and its elements were reviewed and enhanced by scholars in related fields. There was a lot of study that went into it. It wasn't just somebody who had a love of music and could convey that, which is indeed true; but that is true of all music programs. The language element of this one, the developmental aspect of it, is much richer than a music program, per se. So the integration of music, movement, and language is a very different prospect than just music. And her intellectual background in music, coupled with her ability to incorporate pioneers in related fields, from, say Montessori, to neurology, to cognitive development, to literacy skills— her ability to go from the experiential indicators to enriching the curriculum—her ability, with the input from Audrey Sillick, to have the foresight to have environmental sensitivity built in for children at a time prior to this global awareness that is now so engaging—it predated the more recent recognition that the earth is alive and that children are going to inherit it, and they needed to have a sense of relationship to it. This was built into her curriculum ten years before that hit the scene. So it had some incredible foresight. And it's just now becoming as highly relevant as it could be, because it was an answer long before people recognized there was a question.
>
> So, I think admiring the scholarship of it and admiring her credentials and her ability to

collaborate—because it isn't just all her credentials. There were a lot of scholarly contributions that were made. Her ability to take that information— to learn what these people had to offer her and breathe it into the design was really amazingly flexible.

So what we have is an intellectual offering that has a great deal of integrity—it has a real contribution to development. It should be utilized in education—in schools—because it has the academic ground underneath it. It's not just "here's a program—here's how you do it—" but rather "here's a body of lore and here's what it would look like if you deliver it to children in a package that it is based on music." (D. Coulter, personal communication, August 9, 2010)

Lorna's legacy includes the *Musikgarten* early childhood music and movement program, the professional association that is now known as the Early Childhood Music and Movement Association, the *Early Childhood Connections* professional journal (1995–2005), and the Foundation for Music-Based Learning. *Musikgarten* and the teachings through the Foundation continue to enhance the lives of young children and their families with the rich song from the heart of Lorna Lutz Heyge.

APPENDIX

LORNA HEYGE'S PHILOSOPHICAL-POINT DETAILS FROM INTERVIEWS

In the *Musikgarten Messenger* article (Heyge 1999), the *Keyboard Companion* interview (Johnson 2006), and the *Perspectives* interview (Hannagan 2010), Heyge made important philosophical statements that speak of many of her concerns regarding early childhood music and movement.

From the 1999 *Musikgarten Messenger* article:

> Martha Hallquist [editor, *Early Childhood Connections*] says it best, I think, in the Fall 1999 issue of *Early Childhood Connections:* 'Common sense and research suggest that what children consume—whether the foods they eat, the sounds they hear, or the sights they see—affects their development ... let us remind parents that children are affected by the quality of music and literature they hear, read, and watch. Let us stand united in offering children music of the highest quality— whether it be Mozart or folk literature that has survived generations. Will this make our children smarter? Perhaps or perhaps not. Will this enrich our children's lives? Definitely....

> Fine teaching is built on knowledge in three
> primary areas: music, early childhood development,
> and the artistry of teaching. (Heyge 1999)

From the *Keyboard Companion* article (Heyge in Johnson 2006):
There are a number of concepts and principles that I have found to be vitally important:

- All children are musical. Children are innately musical and have an inborn ability to sing and move rhythmically. Research and experience tell us that the earlier a child is in an environment of active music-making, the more likely it is that the child's inborn musicality will be awakened and developed.
- Music-making belongs in the family. The *time* to start experiencing music is in early childhood: the *place* is in the family. Home is the first and most important school for children, and involved parents are the most effective teachers. Music offers parents the simple joys of being together and playing with each other, and encourages them to trust their own natural instincts.
- Music meets the needs of children. Music-making is active and joyful! Psychological studies tell us that a child's primary learning motivation comes from being in a pleasant and non-threatening environment. Songs, rhymes and dances for musical play are time-tested activities which come from our culture and naturally attract children through their beauty and their possibilities for movement and imagination.
- Music makes a difference. Music improves overall development, decreases learning problems, and enhances brain functioning—all in a learning environment that fosters the building of community. Through music we touch the whole child and can make a positive impact on the child and family.
- Movement is essential to learning, and especially to learning music. The human body needs to move in order to develop rhythmic acuity and expression. Without sufficient

movement experience, children do not have the foundation in body control and expressivity to play an instrument. Best of all, movement is exhilarating, energizing and thoroughly enjoyable for children.

- Listening is the most important sensory channel for learning. Focused listening is a casualty of our hectic lives. The very best training for listening requires an emphasis on singing, chanting, and body movement; these link the auditory and vestibular levels of the listening ear. Listening is critical for building the necessary musical connections that allow "music in the head" to be carried to an instrument.

- Children deserve only the most worthwhile music. The songs of childhood are remembered for life. They must be *worth* remembering—songs of musical, textual and cultural value. (Heyge in Johnson 2006)

In the 1970s the approach to early childhood music was good but overly cognitive.[30] In the 1980s we were especially concerned with developmentally appropriate early childhood practice and learned about the deep need for movement in music instruction.

The 1990s, sometimes called the decade of the brain, introduced us to exciting neuroscience research and practice. Our horizons expanded constantly, and our field was especially well suited to adopt holistic practice. In this decade we see a deeply changed society; a society confused about family, education and community; a busy, lonely society. In our day "edutainment" passes for education. Ours are very challenging times for teachers and parents, as well as for trainers, authors and publishers. Our society values *things*, makes a political potato of education, and gives hardly more than lip service to arts education. Presently we have a solid body of knowledge about children and how they learn

---

[30] From my 2011 interview with Linda Robinson: [Kindermusik in 1975] "was very much based the Glockenspiel [as] the main instrument ... that was the note-reading ... that was their way of getting to reading the notation ... what we would do is mark the C and start with C and A—it was their method of teaching notation ... [Lorna] did a whole reverse on how you teach reading and writing music."

music; our biggest challenge is to educate the adults—both parents and rising teachers—about how children learn, why music is vital, and about children's development in its totality. Our challenge is to bring music to a society that has forgotten their singing voices; to spark the adults' musical being when they have so little active music-making experiences. (Heyge in Johnson 2006)

Teacher education is vital. Allow me to mention some of the major challenges in teacher education today:

- Preserving the passion. Teacher education and parent education need to be at the center of our attention. Fortunately many young persons want to teach. We search to find ways to help them keep their passion while we help them gain the many skills they will need for the difficult work that teaching is today—and enable them to earn a living doing it. Passion is what the young often bring us, and without passion there is no place to go! We are challenged to harness that passion so that teachers can be effective and not burn out.

- Filling in the gaps. Because the society in which they have grown up is lacking in active music-making and a true understanding of childhood, young teachers come to us unprepared for the broad aspects of teaching young children. You cannot be *overeducated* for working with children! Since the children's lives are whole, the adults who work with them must approach them holistically. This requires knowledge and experience in many fields, together with fine powers of observation.

- Creating quality, effective teaching materials. In my opinion, good teaching materials need to offer a balance of structure and flexibility *of only worthwhile materials*. Structure gives the young teacher a secure place to start; flexibility offers the teacher a place to grow with experience and study; quality materials make it worthwhile for both teacher and students. In today's entertainment society we must fight for good materials. It is possible, and it is worth the fight! Parents, with our help, learn to appreciate high quality materials. Parent education—and stamina!—are necessary. (Heyge in Johnson 2006)

I am passionate about children and music! Sitting on the floor with children is a wonderful way to spend your life with music. I have the gift of meaningful work and hope to pass it on! Working for the good of children is more important than ever before. Through music we can help foster Community. I recently heard an architect talk about what messages our houses send to the world. Houses fronted by garages rather than porches tell us that "3 cars live here." Houses with privacy fences and elaborate entertainment centers tell us "I have everything I need here; leave me alone." Houses full of computer programs and web access that takes us around the world at the flick of a mouse tell us "I can work and play on my lonely island; everything is need is here."

As much as we all enjoy the advances of technology and increased wealth, we suffer (most unknowingly) from the lack of connection. How wonderful it feels to us as adults to join others to make music. Let us not deny our children this same opportunity.

Music is for ALL children. As music teachers in this society, we work predominantly with the twice-blessed children, those whose parents seek music experience for their children, *and* have sufficient income to pay for it. We must strive to widen the circle of children who can benefit from music.

Movement and listening are two of children's greatest needs today—and music is an ideal vehicle for getting this experience. Children today sit in front of computers, televisions, videos; they sit in car seats, being toted from hither to yon; they play inside because of the lack of safe neighborhood playing-on-the-street opportunities. When do they learn to control their bodies and develop coordination, comfort, rhythm and grace? Children's natural urge to move is frequently overlooked and is vastly underestimated and undervalued in our present way of life.

Children today live in a noise-filled society. There is always sound: iPod/DVD/TV/radio. When do the children focus on a single sound source, give it attention and perceive it? When do they listen to silence, to themselves, to their thoughts, to the music in their heads?

A good teacher + children + a repertoire of singing and dancing games is a formula to develop the movement and listening skills children need.

We need a common repertoire of shared music ... Without it we cannot celebrate the bond music creates in us. We need a common repertoire of songs, so that every piano teacher in America can have the joy of being the magical person who shows the child how to play the tune s/he loves, the tune friends and family know and love. I call this the "Jingle Bells effect."

I have come to deeply admire the wisdom of Shinichi Suzuki, who gave students a set repertoire and advised them to keep an active performance repertoire starting at the elementary level. When Suzuki students come together, they always enjoy playing together.

I listen attentively when I hear elders talk about starting the school day with a singing assembly. Making music together is powerful for the spirit and the mind—to do it we need something we all know!

We must take the needs of parents seriously; they seek the best for their children. We have good news for parents, administrators and politicians. Music is joyful, important to good health and learning, and doesn't require a lot of expensive hardware! In our time of "edutainment" and "infotainment," "in-depth" TV reports that are two minutes in length, and other smoke-screens called education, parents need to hear our message that singing, dancing and talking with their children is very nutritious brain food—one of the best educational advantages they can give their children. Parents need an antidote to the never-ending barrage of commercial messages.

Our responsibility is to constantly work at understanding how children learn—and to be able to communicate that message to parents. "Trust me," is not enough! (Heyge in Johnson 2006)

From the *Perspectives* article (Hannagan 2010):

When I reflect on what I have witnessed over the years, the most notable change is the individual growth of teachers in this field. It is wonderful to see teachers develop, to leave the world of toys and props, and really get down to the basics of how to engage children in what they need. It is encouraging to see so many people really wish to understand the importance of music and movement in the development of the child, and to realize that one of our most important missions is to educate parents – not just please them. Yes, we must please the parents if we hope to build a relationship with them, and we have to meet them where they are, but once that is established, we need to help them grow in their understanding of what children need in terms of both general/academic learning and music learning. In order to do that, we must continually grow in our own understanding. (Heyge in Hannagan 2010)

Hannagan: Looking back from 40 years in the field, what differences have you noticed in the children over the years?

Heyge: I see great differences in society—and therefore, in parents, and in children. Children need more and more of our special gifts that can be given through active music making. They need purposeful movement. They need to develop the ability to listen. They need to refine their singing voices and bodies into expressive, graceful instruments. They need to have their curiosity cultivated through true interaction with the environment and with others in their lives. They already spend too much time just sitting and watching. If I could only deliver one sentence to the teachers and parents spending time with our young children today, I would say: "Put away all of the props, toys, and 'teaching aids' and just be with the children." (Hannagan 2010)

REFERENCES

Cole, Judith W. "Rudolf Laban: Master of Movement." *Early Childhood Connections: Journal of Music-and Movement-Based Learning* 6, no. 3 (2000): 35–39.

Coulter, Dee Joy. *Brain's Timetable for Developing Musical Skills.* Longmont, CO: Coulter Publications, 1982/1994.

Coulter, Dee Joy. "Music and the Making of Mind." *Early Childhood Connections: Journal of Music- and Movement-Based Learning* 1, no. 1 (1995): 22–26.

Coulter, Dee Joy. "Defending the Magic: Current Issues in Early Childhood Education." *Early Childhood Connections: Journal of Music- and Movement-Based Learning* 2, no. 2 (1996): 30–35.

Coulter, Dee Joy. "Mind and Music in the 21ˢᵗ Century." *Early Childhood Connections: Journal of Music- and Movement-Based Learning* 6, no. 1 (2000): 9–12.

Crain, William. *Theories of Development: Concepts and Applications* (5ᵗʰ ed). Upper Saddle River, NJ: Pearson Education, Inc., 2005.

Gettman, David. *Basic Montessori: Learning Activities for Under-Fives.* New York: St. Martin's Press, 1987.

Gordon, Edwin E. "Pattern Preeminence in Learning Music." *Early Childhood Connection: Journal of Music- and Movement-Based Learning,* 10, no. 2 (2004): 7–13.

Hallquist, Martha. "Leadership Bulletin: A New Day is Dawning." *Early Childhood Connections: Journal of Music- and Movement-Based Learning* 6, no. 1 (2000): 58.

Hallquist, Martha. "Leadership Bulletin: Patterns that Connect." *Early Childhood Connections: Journal of Music- and Movement-Based Learning* 10, no. 2 (2004): 60.

Hannagan, Jill Citro. "Getting to Know You: Lorna Heyge." *Perspectives* 5, no. 2 (2010).

Heyge, Lorna. "Commentary." *Early Childhood Connections: Journal of Music- and Movement-Based Learning* 1, nos. 1, 2 (1995): 5–13.

Heyge, Lorna. "Foundation for Music-Based Learning Founded by Lorna and Hermann Heyge." *Early Childhood Connections: Journal of Music- and Movement-Based Learning* 1, nos. 1, 2 (1995b): 51.

Heyge, Lorna. "A Musical Journey." *Musikgarten Messenger.* Greensboro, NC: Music Matters, Inc. (1999).

Heyge, Lorna. "ECC Salutes Audrey Sillick." *Early Childhood Connections: Journal of Music- and Movement-Based Learning* 5, no. 3 (1999b): 6.

Heyge, Lorna. "The Nation's Pride: Celebrating Head Start's 35th Birthday." *Early Childhood Connections: Journal of Music- and Movement-Based Learning* 6, no. 4 (2000): 30-35.

Heyge, Lorna. "The Well-Prepared Beginner: Prepared in Body, Mind, Spirit, and Family." *Early Childhood Connections: Journal of Music- and Movement-Based Learning* 8, no. 1 (2002): 28–33.

Heyge, Lorna. "An Open Letter to Readers from ECC Publisher, Lorna Heyge." *Early Childhood Connections: Journal of Music- and Movement-Based Learning* 11, no. 2 (2005): 58.

Heyge, Lorna. (2011). 40th-Anniversary Reminiscence: Transcription of Speech Given at *Musikgarten* Festival, April 29, 2011.

Heyge, Lorna, Jill Citro Hannagan, and Mary Louise Wilson. *Music Makers: At the Keyboard.* Greensboro, NC: Music Matters, Inc., 2001.

Heyge, Lorna, Jill Citro Hannagan, and Mary Louise Wilson. *Music Makers: At the Keyboard—Parent Guide.* Greensboro, NC: Music Matters, Inc., 2001b.

Heyge, Lorna, and Audrey Sillick. *Teacher's Guide, Year One: Kindermusik for the Very Young.* Walton, New York: Music Resources International, 1988.

Heyge, Lorna, and Audrey Sillick. *Musikgarten Music and Movement Series: The Cycle of Seasons.* Greensboro, NC: Musikgarten/Music Matters, Inc., 2007.

Heyge, Lorna, and Audrey Sillick. *Musikgarten Music and Movement Series Family Music: Volume 2: Play with Me—Clap with Me.* Greensboro, NC: Musikgarten/Music Matters, Inc., 2003.

Heyge, Lorna, and Audrey Sillick. *Musikgarten Music and Movement Series Family Music for Babies: Teacher's Guidebook.* Greensboro, NC: Music Matters, Inc., 1997.

Heyge, Lorna, and Audrey Sillick. "Music: A Natural Way to Play with Babies." *Early Childhood Connections: Journal of Music- and Movement-Based Learning* 4, no. 4 (1998): 8–13.

Johnson, Rebecca. "Teaching the Young Child: An Interview with Lorna Heyge." *Keyboard Companion* 17, no. 3 (2006): 34–37.

Jordan-DeCarbo, Joyce. "Early Childhood Music Education: Reflections on the Past and Projections for the Future." *Early Childhood Connections: Journal of Music- and Movement-Based Learning* 10, no. 1 (2004): 35–44.

Jordan-DeCarbo, Joyce. "Growing with *Early Childhood Connections:* A Reviewer's Reflections." *Early Childhood Connections: Journal of Music- and Movement-Based Learning* 11, no. 2 (2005): 43-44.

Keene, James A. *A History of Music Education in the United States* (2nd ed.). Centennial, CO: Glenbridge Publishing Ltd., 2009.

Lillard, Paula Polk. *Montessori Today: A Comprehensive Approach to Education from Birth to Adulthood.* New York: Schocken Books, 1996.

Lineburgh, Nancy E. (2000). "Kodály and Early Childhood Music." *Early Childhood Connections: Journal of Music- and Movement-Based Learning* 6, no. 3 (2000): 22–28.

Linkins, Jean Ellen. *The Pedagogical Philosophy of Lorna Lutz Heyge, PhD.* Unpublished dissertation, Bob Jones University, 2012.

Mark, Michael L. "Unique Aspects of Historical Research in Music Education." *The Bulletin of Historical Research in Music Education* 6, no. 1 (1985): 29–33. Accessed February 11, 2010. http://www.jstor.org/stable/40214680.

Maubach, Christoph. "Introduction to the Orff Schulwerk Approach." (2006) Victorian (Australia) Orff Schulwerk website. Accessed February 11, 2012, http://www.vosa.org/aboutorff/.

McDonald, Dorothy T., and Gene M. Simons. *Musical Growth and Development.* New York: Schirmer Books, 1989.

Morrison, George S. *Early Childhood Education Today* (9th ed.). Upper Saddle River, NJ: Pearson/Merrill Prentice Hall, 2004.

Nash, Grace. C. *Creative Approaches to Child Development with Music, Language and Movement: Incorporating the Philosophies and Techniques of Orff, Kodaly, and Laban.* Port Washington, NY: Alfred Publishing Company, Inc., 1974.

Piaget, Jean, and Bärbel Inhelder. *The Psychology of the Child.* New York: Basic Books, 2000.

Puckett, Margaret B., and Deborah Diffily. *Teaching Young Children: An Introduction to the Early Childhood Profession* (2nd ed.). Clifton Park, NY: Delmar Learning, 2004.

Sillick, Audrey. "Montessori's Gift: One Teacher's Point of View." *Early Childhood Connections: Journal of Music- and Movement-Based Learning* 1, no. 3 (1995): 22–25.

Standing, Edwin Mortimer. *Maria Montessori: Her Life and Her Work.* New York: Plume, 1998.

Wucher, Diethard. "Celebrating 25 years of Early Childhood Music Education in Germany." *Early Childhood Connections: Journal of Music- and Movement-Based Learning* 2, no. 1 (1996): 5–11.

INDEX

O

Orff, Carl 16, 22, 23, 36, 42, 63,
64, 84, 85

P

parent and family involvement
49, 67
Pestalozzi, Johann Heinrich 22,
26, 67
PhD in Musicology 5
Piaget, Jean 22, 25, 28, 29, 30,
31, 67, 85

R

Robinson, Linda xvi, 11, 16, 20,
65, 75
Rousseau, Jean-Jacques 22, 25,
67
Rucker, Amy xvi, 13, 35, 36, 37

S

Schneider, Michael 5
Sheets, Donna xvi
Sheppard, Melissa xvi
Sillick, Audrey xvi, 12, 23, 32, 37,
39, 64, 67, 82
solfège 23, 37
Spickard, Jeff 21
Stellvertretende Direktor 7
synthesis xi, 51

T

teacher-trainers 14, 21, 23, 30,
38, 52, 53
teacher-training workshop 11,
14, 16
teaching artistry 22, 30, 49, 51,
52, 53, 54, 67
The Neuroscience of Music 43, 44
The Ways Children Learn Music
Bluestine, Eric 46
Tina und Tobi 8
Toronto 11, 12, 14, 32, 37, 39, 63,
64
Toth, Barb 16
Troisdorf 7, 67
Turner, Dan xvi

U

University of Cologne 4, 5
University of Rochester 2, 4

W

Walcha, Helmut 4
Wilson, Mary Louise xvi, 13, 15,
60, 61
Wucher, Diethard 8, 9, 28, 55, 57,
58, 59, 85

Printed in the United States
By Bookmasters